American Democracy 2.0

Bypassing Our Broken Government

BY

Manuel "Manny" Fernandez

Contents

4

1.American Democracy 2.0

American Democracy 2.0 is a remarkable process given to the people by the constitution that provides passing amendments while bypassing our broken, partisan, uncompromising government.

No longer will the people have to suffer inaction by the government when they hold marches and rallies on issues such as gun control.

The process proceeds in a democratic sequence of events as follows.

The state legislatures vote for a convention to pass amendments. A vote of two-thirds of the state legislatures (34 -to- 50) is required to approve the convention.

While not spelled out in the constitution, the convention should be called for

specific amendments (such as Gun Control, Healthcare and Abortion Rights).

The strong force that guided me in this initiative guided me to recommend specific details on amendments that could be written and I present them for consideration. However, as will be discussed, the written amendments to be voted on and the results of the voting will be determined by the people, not by what I recommend.

Once the convention is approved, the process can proceed as follows.

Selected Law schools, from those showing interest in specific issues, will write the amendments. For example, one law school will write the recommended amendment for the pro-life group and another law school will write the recommended amendment for the pro-choice group. Note that this process avoids the partisan rhetoric that seldom states the clear positions of the arguing groups.

The next step is for selected college debating societies, from those expressing interest in specific issues, to hold public debates on prime-time national TV. The pro-choice team would have 40 minutes to present their position. Then the prolife team would have 30 minutes to present their reply to the pro-choice's presentation. Finally, the pro-choice team would have 20 minutes to respond to the reply. Then the pro-life would follow similarly. Note that this procedure in contrast to the 90 second statement and the 30 second response followed by past TV debates which have not been effective in coming to a conclusion on the issues.

Polling of the people will follow the debate with the technique followed by American Idol which recorded 60 million votes in a few hours. Note that this contrasts with past polls wherein only 1,000 votes were counted.

The final step is for the state legislatures to vote. Note that a pass requires a vote of three-fourths of the state legislatures (38 -to- 50). Note that both amendments could fail to pass.

The process is of the people, for the people and by the people.

It is important that written amendments be available so that the people are clear of what the polling and voting is about.

It is important that the debates be specific. In this regard, referees will be available to ensure that debaters not state false or misleading statements.

It is important for the polling to be held. The state legislatures will not be held to the results of the polling.

While not yet allowed by the constitution, I recommend that a new amendment be passed that allows state legislatures to hold a convention to pass laws. This would be similar to the amendment to pass amendments. I recommend this because many national problems can be resolved better with laws rather than amendments.

I present recommendations on how to resolve twenty-one national problems, as follows.

Gun Control

Healthcare

Creating Jobs

Improving the Economy

Fixing the Supreme Court

Fixing Congress

Fixing the Executive Branch

Fixing Federal Elections

Fixing Partisan Politics

Fixing Federal Deficits

Fixing the Federal Debt

Tax Reform

Subprime Loans

Solving the Foreclosure Problem

Social Security

Medicare

Trade

Fixing the Immigration Crisis

Proving Tuition-Free College Education

Abortion Rights

America Corps

Amendment on Passing Laws

A very important anticipated result of the process is that today's divided society will become more united on issues, thus allowing resolution of national problems.

I feel I have an obligation to all individual Americans and to the entire country to reveal to them what the strong force that guided me to a course of action that can be taken to solve the nation's major problems by bypassing the obstacles that in effect gridlocks today's governmental processes.

While I have listed candidate amendments to be considered that involve national problems that need resolution and/or fixing of our Federal government, fixing our Federal elections and/or fixing partisan politics, our constitution should be amended to include rights and values

This is truly a democratic process written in the constitution involving a large, diversified population of interests. These participants are contributing to improve the future of individual Americans and to the future of the entire country. Participants in the process can be trusted. College students are included in writing the amendments and debating the amendments. There is no room for special interests to dominate because of power, authority or influence. The average America would only have to be knowledgeable on the amendments, hear the debates, vote and abide with the results of the vote.

Because our present three branches of government cannot be counted on to manage the proposed process, it is suggested that a fourth branch of government be established to manage the process. We will call this branch the America Corps. It will have no authority. It will simply manage the process. It will suggest to the state legislatures to vote on a convention to consider specific amendments. It will select law schools and college debating societies expressing interest to participate. It will arrange for dissemination of written amendments, the debates themselves, the polling, the results of the polling and the tally of votes by the state legislatures.

The America Corps will be composed of a group of annual governor's appointments of a recent college graduate to serve a two-year paid term. In the steady state, there will be 100 members serving. The members will have support teams to carry out their responsibilities. They will select a management team to serve a one-year term. Some members will be involved in managing the process as discussed above. Other members will work to provide solutions to national problems. If the America Corps management concludes that some of these solutions deserve action, they can disseminate them to the public and to the state legislatives in order that they can be considered to be part of the process. And let me make it clear that our country has many, many more national problems then the twenty that are discussed here (e.g., education, the environment, etc.). Readers should note that it is recommended that the number of House members and Senators be reduced from 535 to 118. The addition of the 100 America Corps still is a very large reduction in numbers. The reduction in the number of members of Congress also supports the need for the America Corps who will supplement only one of the responsibilities of Congress (the recommending of amendments to the constitution, which Congress seems not to pursue vigorously), but not take away any responsibilities given to Congress by the constitution.

Since it will take time to have a working America Corps as discussed, there is a need for a non-government organization to be established immediately to kick off the process. Hopefully, some wealthy individuals will endow such an organization.

Readers should keep in mind that the process provides a level of understanding of the issues that is not available to Americans today or that has been available in the past. Clearly, Americans seldom were totally aware of the details of the written legislation, the issues debated and the pros and cons raised by the legislation. Special Interests spent millions on media campaigns to advocate for their side of the issues. Further, Americans were never polled effectively as to their support to the extent proposed in the recommendation. My hope is that in support of this initiative, that all Americans will become more active and more participative in government affairs. This includes registering to vote and voting in all elections and participating in the recommended initiative. If the initiative is successful, this will add to this change. This will eliminate the wide division between warring groups in today's society.

The amendment to proposing laws is provided to cover solutions which do not fit amendments as they fit better to be incorporated into laws. This amendment is meant to allow for a convention to pass laws similar to the existing amendment allowing conventions for proposing amendments. There are many issues with state laws that are not consistent among states that could become consistent at a national level. This is not to disallow states to have the right to pass laws.

History will record whether a once successful democracy, now broken, can be fixed and saved and grow and improve with the will of the people united in a cause to fix what is wrong. Keep in mind that a process has been recommended whose results will be determined by the people, for the people and of the people. It is hoped that solutions will be accepted by 90 % of the people and that this unity of action will end the warring between the two divided sides of today's society. Review the twenty solutions and decide on your own if they could be popular to the extent hoped for.

Visit us at

Americacorps.online

2.0 Gun Control

When I read Amendment II of the Constitution, I realized that the amendment does not provide any rights to all of today's citizens to keep and bear arms.

I fault the Supreme Court for not making this clear to the country, especially when the issue was so publicly debated.

Here's the Amendment:

AMENDMENT II
Right to Bear Arms

A well-regulated Militia, being necessary to the security of a free-state, the right of the people to keep and bear arms, shall not be infringed.

The Dictionary defines Militia as follows:

1. a part of the organized armed forces of a country liable to call only in an emergency.
2. the whole body of able-bodied male citizens declared by law as being subject to call to military service - militiaman.

In the late 18th century, the country had no standing army. Therefore, in an emergency the country planned to have a Militia to call upon. This required the Militia to be armed on their own without government need to supply arms. Note that the amendment gave a right to bear arms to a select few: The Militia in the 18th and the 19th Centuries. Note that the right was given only to men within the ages selected to be included in the Militia; no women.

Cleary, our country today has an armed military and does not have authority to call citizens into military service (we have a volunteer military). Therefore, Amendment II was viable only for the conditions of the 19th century, but not for today's situation. In fact, Amendment II should be removed as no longer valid in today's situation. A new Amendment should be passed to suit today's circumstances.

Let me hasten to say that only a vote of three-fourths of the State legislatures can amend the
Constitution. Per Article V, two thirds (34 of 50 States) can call a Convention for proposing **Amendments**. Ratification then requires three fourths (38 of 50 States) voting for Amendments.

I caution Americans not to let the Executive Branch, nor Congress, pass a law or institute regulations that will substitute for a Constitutional amendment that defines what rights Americans have to keep and bear arms and includes what gun control measures are required to protect against mass shootings.

As I pointed out in the Preface, I recommend debates, polling and votes by the state legislatures to include a substitute amendment on the right to bear arms. In reality, the vote would be for or against two substitute amendments to be debated. A vote of 38 (or more) -to-50 is required for an amendment to pass. Keep in mind that both substitute amendments could fail to pass. This is a democratic process guaranteed by the constitution.

Many Americans have recommended that the constitution should be changed to reduce the effects of mass shootings (the number of people killed and the number of people injured). This would involve making it illegal to own a gun with a high rate of fired bullets per minute and the clips that provide this high rate to continue for a long period. There is no argument that this will achieve the recommended objective to reduce the effects of mass shootings. The gun lobby argues (falsely) that the constitution does not allow restrictions and (falsely) that recommended changes would not prevent mass shootings (which is not the recommendation).

There are also issues to be debated involving reducing the number of mass shootings. There are recommendations that could help reduce the number of mass shootings (not eliminate them entirely), the gun lobby (falsely) argues that guns are not a factor in this issue. Clearly, a shooter would not engage in a mass shooting if he/she did not have the means to affect the mass shootings planned.

Americans have not been provided with effective debates on the issues. The process recommended will provide effective debates.

3.0 Healthcare

I was driven by a strong force to write this medical healthcare plan and to publish it as a contribution to the national debate on repealing and replacing Obamacare.

In 2014, the government (Federal and State) spent $615.3 billion on healthcare programs for 90 million Americans eligible for these programs (Medicaid $492.3 billion; CHIP $13 billion; Obamacare $110 billion).

The plan has a premium of $40 per month and covers catastrophic medical expenses up to $350,000 annually with a lifetime cap of $1,500,000. This a plan to avoid financial disasters or bankruptcy. At the same time, the plan is a healthcare plan that has a low $2,000 deductible and a low out-of-pocket maximum of $8,000.

The plan has full coverage for physician, hospital, prescription drugs, and limited coverage for other services (vision, dental, hearing and gym membership).

Payments to providers will be set a 150% of Medicare payments with a low 30% co-pay after the deductible. If the retail price is $200 and the payment is set at $150, beneficiaries will only have to pay a co-pay of $45 for a savings of $155 after the deductible period and a saving of $50 during the deductible period. These savings help pay for the Premiums. In this example, the government pays zero, the policyholder pays $45 and the insurer pays $105.

With the payment set at $150, many providers will accept this plan in contrast to Medicaid.

Prescription drug prices will be negotiated by the government thus providing additional savings to the beneficiaries during and after the deductible period. This also helps covering the cost of the premiums.

This plan would be available to the 90 million Americans on Medicaid, CHIP, Obamacare.

The plan would lower government costs (Federal and State) by $133.3 billion annually. This is based on an average of $4,105 of claims. No longer will states have to pay for Medicaid.

Others may choose to apply. For example, a similar, but different, plan would be available to employers for the benefit of their employees with a limit set on the out-of-pocket limit of $8,000. The cost to the employer would be $8,272 per year, vs the present cost of $18,000 in California.

Contrast this to what we are told that our present healthcare system is the highest cost compared to other countries and that our healthcare benefits are the lowest of other countries. Clearly, the recommended plan reverses these dire metrics.

The way the plan will work is that Obamacare would not be repealed. Americans would choose between this plan and Obamacare. Insurers will be given the chance to make their Obamacare policies competitive. However, since this plan is so much better than Obamacare, it is expected that Americans will choose this plan and that insurers will drop their Obamacare policies and thus end Obamacare.

The plan would pay individuals qualified for government subsidies for 100% of the premiums and deductible. Prescriptions and co-pays are not covered. Not covering the cost of prescription drugs and co-pays is an incentive to have these insured take responsibilities for their personal health. It is also an incentive to seek a job that provides employee healthcare benefits.

There would no reduction in present coverage for those now on Medicaid.

Hospital care will be free for the first 60 days, with a co-pay of $100 per day for the next 60 days after the first 60 days. After the second 60-day period, the insured would pay the total hospital bill. This is meant to foster better healthcare by providers to minimize hospital stays. As with Medicare, multiple 60-day free periods will be allowed if separated by non-hospital periods of 60 days.

Half of the excess revenue will be contributed to a national charity to help beneficiaries that are approaching their annual benefit limits or their lifetime cap limits. If unused, the remaining excess revenue will be saved and invested as surplus assets.

The reason the plan is so effective is that the cost is low, thus drawing a large payer base, most of which are healthy and thus submit no or small claims. The other reason is that the plan provides excellent healthcare thus providing heathy clients which results in no or small claims.

Individuals on Medicare would like to join the recommended plan and pay only $420 per month and be protected up to $350,000 annually with only a $2,000 deductible. To avoid this, those eligible for Medicare would have to be enrolled in Medicare to be able to join the plan and receive benefits. Also, Medicare would be the primary coverage before the recommended plan accepts claims.

The plan will not accept an individual with a pre-existing condition. Therefore, Americans will sign up to the low $420 per month premium before they develop a pre-existing condition. The policyholders that have low claims will be paying for the benefits of those policyholders that have high claims. Individuals with a pre-existing condition that are insured would be allowed to switch plans and be covered. It is not fair for an individual to not buy insurance until he/she develops a pre-existing medical condition and be accepted. Individuals will not be dropped if they get sick. Individuals will not be allowed to drop this plan and reapply later when they develop a preexisting medical condition. A grace period will be allowed for individuals who have a pre-existing medical condition and are presently uninsured to apply and be accepted. **Clearly, all Americans with a pre-existing condition will be initially accepted.**

The objective of the plan is to make America the healthiest country in the world with the best healthcare in the world. The result should achieve the lowest per captia cost in the world as progress is made towards these objectives.

There will be no network providers.

Note that all members will receive the same superior medical care thus helping achieve the objective to make the country the healthiest country in the world.

A national charitable organization will be set up to provide a sustainable medical/financial regimen for individuals who are nearing their annual and/or lifetime benefit limit/cap and to provide financial aid when these limits/caps are exceeded. Contributions to the organization will be solicited from public/private sources. This plan will contribute 50% of its surplus revenue for these causes.

The plan will be offered by a Federally-Chartered Corporation with Trustees from past Presidents.

Compare this plan with the unacceptable plans put forward by the GOP-led House and Senate.

This plan avoids the problems with Obamacare (high premiums and deductibles) and avoids the problems with Trump Obamacare (reduced coverage and higher premiums and deductibles, reduced coverage for Medicaid eligibility, less subsidies, less coverage for pre-existing conditions, etc.).

This plan should receive support by the Democrats because it doesn't repeal Obamacare and the plan should receive support from the Republicans because it saves $392.3billion annually and provides a Trump plan acceptable to all Americans supporting his stated objective.

The reason the plan is so effective is that it attracts a huge base of healthy insured that help pay for the costs to care for those insured with high claims.

The program can be known as Americare.

Those under Medicaid, CHIP and Obamacare will receive benefits for premiums and deductible totaling $2,480. In addition, they receive savings on services and prescription drugs and other services.
Those under employee programs will receive benefits for premiums ($420/month), deductible ($2,000) and co-pays.
In addition, they will receive savings on services and prescription drugs and other services. There will be a similar plan available to the general public, the now 28 million unemployed.

Those under Medicare will receive savings on services and prescription drugs and other services, they will pay premiums of $420/month.

The cost to the government of $615.3 billion will be reduced to zero.
All insurered will have the annual $350,000 catastrophic coverage and the lifetime catastrophic coverage of $1,500,000. All will have a low co-pay of 30% and an out of pocket maximum of $8,000.

It is estimated that the 348 million policies will have claims of $4,105 per policy on average which equates to $1,000 billion total benefits paid on an annual basis. The $4,105 claim equates to an average co-pay of $1,232 (30%) and an average benefit of $2,873 (70%). The estimated Financial Summary is shown below.

Estimated Financial Summary (in billions)

Premiums (P), Deductibles (D), Co-Pays (C), Benefits (B)

Policies	Insured Pays	Insurer Pays	Employer Pays	Government Pays	Policies	
Medicaid {	$111 (C)	$892 (P,D,B)	0	0		
CHIP {						
Obamacare {					90 million	
Employees	0	460 (B)	$1,324 (P,D,C)	0	160 million	
Uninsured	232 (P,D,C)	80 (B)	0	0	28 million	
Medicare	579 (P,D,C)	201 (B)	0	0	70 million	
Total (B)	$922	$1,633	$1,324	0	348 million	$1,000

Note, the total spent is $3,879 billion. There is no cost to the government (State or Federal).

Income is $1,300 billion, Benefits paid are $1,223 billion for a profit of $77 billion.

This leaves a balance of $77 billion to be allocated as shown below

Reserve to cover higher Claims	$62 billion
Operating Costs	5
Excess Reserve	10
Total	$77 billion

Half of the Excess Reserve ($5 billion) will be donated to a charitable organization as discussed above to aid policy holders with high claims.

Note that there is an annual savings of $615.3 to the government (Federal and State) now spent on Medicaid, CHIP and Obamacare.

Membership is voluntary. Americans and employers can choose from plans available.

Note that there is zero cost to the government (Federal and State).

Clearly, this is a plan that is much, much better than "Medicare For All".

Also, it is a better plan than is available today from Obamacare or private plans.

Special interests will want to kill this plan. Here are possible criticisms and rebuttals.

This is a single payer plan; no, it is not because all other plans are allowed.

This is a public option. No, it is not. It is a Corporate (Federally Chartered) offered plan. The Trustees are past Presidents. The government has no control of this Corporation's plan.

It will kill private plans. No, it will not as Americans and employers can choose from plans available.

It will kill "Medicare For All". Yes, it will unless the government fixes Medicare problems.

Employees will be forced to give up their plans. No, they will not because they and their employers will have a choice of what plans are available. Membership is voluntary.

It will do away with Medicaid, CHIP and Obamacare. No it will not because those plans will be choices available to those qualified.

4.0 Creating Jobs and Improving the Economy

The $615.3 billion annually in savings provided by the healthcare replacement plan can be used to create six million jobs the first year and for years into the future for infrastructure/public works projects. Local governments would propose projects and the Federal government would provide 80% - 100% of the funding for approved projects depending on the local unemployment rate and the ability of the local government to pay a share.

The objective is to rehabilitate and renovate communities with projects that bring jobs, improve the economy improve the communities and bring better lives to its people. New jobs would be created with opportunities for employment regarding creative jobs.

The economy can also be improved by providing responsible, easy, low interest rate loans to small businesses startups and to individuals. Unfortunately, the FED provided no- interest loans to large financial institutions but made it impossible for many Americans to obtain low-cost loans. The disappearance of small community banks made it more difficult to secure these needed low-cost loans. These loans will create millions of additional jobs nationwide as new businesses will be established and individuals will contract to improve their properties.

Later, I will recommend actions that will indirectly create jobs and improve the economy. These actions are 1) to eliminate deficits and pay down the Federal debt, 2) eliminate foreclosures, 3) provide a respectful interest rate income from bank accounts, CD's and IRA's and 4) provide needed tax reform.

5.0 Fixing the Supreme Court

The Supreme Court's mission is to protect the Constitutional Rights of Americans. Its mission is not to change the Constitution, make law nor to promote an ideology.

Yet on a decision dealing with age discrimination the Court ruled that it is up to the fired employee to prove that he or she was fired for age discrimination. Prior to this decision, the Federal Courts required the employer to prove that age discrimination was not the cause for firing.

Clearly the above decision does not involve Constitutional Rights. Therefore, the Court should not have heard the case and instead allowed the Federal Courts to decide the case on a case-by-case basis. The decision that changes the law appears to be based on political ideology such as providing Corporate America with protection from such law suits. Further, it promotes the idea that the Court is the highest court in the land and that cases, not involving Constitutional Rights, can be settled by the Court. The counter argument is that the Constitution guarantees a trial by jury and a 5 -to- 4 decision by nine Justices is not a valid substitute for a trial by jury.

This is only one example of similar cases that can only be understood as a give-a-way to Corporate America or other special interest groups.

If a case in Federal Courts involves Constitutional Rights, the Court should be asked to issue a decision only on the Constitutional Rights issues, but not on the case itself. Keep in mind that Federal Courts are knowledgeable concerning Constitutional Rights and can handle those questions without resorting to moving the decision to the Court. Of course, attorneys may argue and endure that it is necessary to move the decision to the Court.

The action of the Court should be to state what the Constitutional Right is and what the Constitution states the Constitutional Right is. Then it should be the action of the Federal Courts to come to a decision on the case since only the Federal Courts can issue a verdict with penalties.

I viewed an old interview of Justice Scalia. In this interview, Justice Scalia stated that the Court is not a policing organization. He went on to state that on cases brought to the Court, the Court's concern is that no one is harmed.

Justice Scalia did not explain in the interview that cases have to be brought to the Court and that the Court alone decides what cases it will hear within the short period it is in session on an annual basis. Readers should understand that a qualified attorney has to be hired to petition the Court for a hearing.

There are many cases wherein the Court has not decided properly and wherein the Court has issued on a decision with a slimmest of margins (5 -to- 4, 55%). I recommend that the Court decides to protect Constitutional Rights and that the margin be 75% (7 -to- 2). I take this stand because I believe that Justices reviewing the Constitution should all come to a more unanimous decision. If this margin is not achieved, there is no decision and the case is left to the Federal Courts to decide on a case-by-case basis. I also recommend that Federal Judges be elected, not nominated by the President and confirmed by the Senate. I also recommend that the Court not be recognized as the highest court in the land by deciding cases moved from the Federal Courts to make a decision on a case not involving Constitutional Rights.

Clearly, from the above, the Court needs reform.

The above deficiencies require reforms as follows:

1. Harm to Americans is not a good criterion for protecting Constitutional Rights. The Court's mission should be to protect Constitutional Rights of all Americans and this objective must be followed by the Court.

2. The Court should simplify how cases are presented to the Court. The Court should reform its process so that it can handle more cases during it session. Also, that its period of operation be a year-long period with a first-come, first-served arrangement.

3. The Court should make a decision on a 75% vote required to pass (7 out of 9 Justices). If this 75% margin is not met, the question is to be settled by the Federal Courts on a case-by-case basis.

Americans are told that our Constitution was set up with three Branches (Congress, the Supreme Court and the Executive Branch) and that this setup provides an important check and balance to the exercise of power.

The fact is that there is no check and balance as Congress has passed laws changing the Constitution, the Court has made law and the Executive Branch has been making law and violating the Constitution by making law through Executive Orders.

The above can be corrected as follows:

1. Each Branch of government be required to publish its action one month before the action is to become effective in order to allow the other two Branches to review and vote their approval or disapproval. Exceptions will be allowed for emergency actions wherein immediate action immediate action is required. A disapproval will stop the proposed action. Readers will note that Americans vote for members of Congress and for elected officials of the Executive Branch (President, and Vice President). Yet the Justices are nominated by the President and confirmed by the Senate. This process has not worked very well because the political parties insist that the Court should be filled with candidates that express the ideology of their own party.

To correct the above the following is recommended:

1. Justices will be elected. Two Justices will be elected each Presidential election until nine elected Justices are sitting on the bench. Presently nominated and confirmed Justices now sitting on the bench and promised lifetime terms will be allowed to serve their lifetime terms or until they pass, resign or are voted out of office. For a time, there will be more than nine Justices sitting on the bench. It will take 20 years before nine elected Justices are sited. Therefore, I recommend considering electing three Justices each Presidential election (instead of two) in order to reduce the 20-year period to 12 years. It will take 20 years or more

for presently nominated and confirmed Justices to be absent from the bench. If a vacancy of an elected Justice occurs, it will be filled during the next Presidential election after at least a nine month period after the vacancy occurs to allow adequate election campaigns for the candidates.

2. All sited Justices will appear on the ballot in every election. A 75% "No" vote will remove a Justice from office.

3. The number of Justices on the Court shall be stated in the Constitution and not subject to a vote by Congress as is now the case.

4. Whereas today's nominees for the Court do not answer questions on their values, the election of Justices will reform this because candidates for election will want to broadcast their values.

5. Keep in mind that Elected Justices will come under the rules of elected officials and that they will have to meet election and campaign financing rules.

I would recommend that consideration be given to spell out such issues as abortion rights, equal-pay rights, etc., and readdress issues such as campaign financing, same sex marriages, etc. and issues facing the country and its people which the Constitution does not address directly (or perhaps shouldn't address). This is a separate issue from fixing the Supreme Court. It is an issue of rewriting the Constitution or amending it.

As always, I recommend that the Law Schools write the new laws and the Constitutional Amendments, that debates be held by college debating societies and that national polling be conducted. In this regard, readers should understand that the Law Schools may change my recommendations, that the debates may bring forth new issues, that the polling will reveal the peoples' opinion and that the votes of the States' Legislatures may reveal whether a Constitutional Amendment will be passed.

I believe that I have made a case for my recommendations. The debates can extend the arguments on both sides of the changes recommended. And the national polling should reveal the support or non-support of the people. Americans should be vigilant that the special interests will try to defeat the efforts to make needed changes from the status quo. This is why Americans should all join the five Boycotts recommended.

Remember that this is all about saving ourselves and our country and fixing our broken government

26

6. Fixing Congress

I have written articles that will help fixing Congress

  Fixing Federal Elections

  Fixing Partisan Politics

This article focuses on other issues that are required to fix Congress.

Changing Federal elections so that there is a single Primary Election and a Final General Election every four years (the years of Presidential Elections). We are eliminating Midterm elections.

  Changing the number of Senators and Representatives for each State.

  Eliminating the Electoral College.

  Reducing Costs while improving the effectiveness of Congress in serving the people and the country.

There are now a total of 100 Senators (two from each State). This is to be reduced to a total of 50 Senators (one from each State).

At present, the smallest States in resident population have a population of 700,000 and qualify for one Representative per State. California with the largest resident population of 39 million has 53 Representatives (one each for each 700,000 in population). In the recommendation, California will have four Representatives, one for each 10,000,000 in population.

One has to consider that the Supreme Court has only nine Justices and has an equal important role amongst the three Branches of the Federal government. These figures do not count the large staffs associated with members of Congress and the Supreme Court.

There are now a total of 435 Representatives. This will be reduced to a total of 58 Representatives. California will have only four Representatives instead of the present 53 Representatives. Most States will have only one Representative as is now the case. A few States, Like Texas, will now have more than one Representative, but not more than three

Representatives. Forty-Four States will now have only one Representative, while six States will have two or more Representatives, but not more than four Representatives.

There will be no term limits.

Salaries of members of Congress (both in the Senate and the House) will be increased. The new salaries will be 80% of the President's salary for Senators and 60% of the President's salary for Representatives. The goal is to attract top candidates and to provide them with a salary that will reject lobbyists' influence.

The bad practices of Re-Districting (for House Seats in each State) will be eliminated by requiring Districts to follow county lines.

All member of Congress will be up for re-election every four years (as the terms of Senators will be reduced from six years to four years).

If there is a vacancy, Governors will be required to appoint replacements, without Federal or State approvals. Such appointments will be required to be made within 30 days, or less, of the vacancy.

Requirements necessary to pass legislation in the Senate and the House will be 75%. No longer will the Senate or the House require a different rule for passing legislation.

Note that we are recommending that the America Corps recommend solutions to national problems, that law schools write Constitutional Amendments and recommended new laws, that college debating societies debate the issues, that national polling be held and that state legislatures vote on them. Clearly, this represents the best practices for a democracy. Note that our top young adults in the America Corps, the law schools and the college debating societies will be participating to improve the country.

Note that I have already recommended solutions to many of the country's problems. Progress on these recommendations can proceed with action from the law schools, the college debating societies and the national polls, in that order.

We expect a reduction in government costs (both Federal and State) from the above recommendations. The CBO is asked to report on this expected cost reduction.

We also expect that Congressional actions will improve due to these and other recommendations made in the aforementioned articles. Note that citizens in 44 States will only have to keep track of how their one Senator and their one Representative vote on issues.

7. FIXING THE EXECUTIVE BRANCH

The Executive Branch has become a large bureaucracy of politically-appointed officials. This is a far cry from the situation existing in the early decades of the country. Of course, the situation today is much more complex because we are a large economy within a larger world economy.

Unfortunately, the Executive Branch is not effectively carrying out its intended purpose to run the country according to the law, providing essential Federal services and promoting economic prosperity and financial security for the country and its people.

It appears that the government is more and more concerned about serving the interests of special interests than the interests of the country and its people.

I recommend that our government seek to reduce this large bureaucracy, improve operations and to reduce costs of operation. This would help to reduce Federal Deficits and to start paying off our Federal Debt.

I don't have to recite the many failings of government agencies like the USDA, the FAA, the FDA, etc. The Executive Branch needs to give attention to obtaining better performance from all of its agencies and Departments. Hopefully, with the elimination of mid-term elections, the Executive Branch can give more attention to this aspect of good governance.

Finally, I believe that the three Branches of government are not working effectively together to serve the people and provide the checks and balances intended by our founding fathers. This should not be an adversary relationship, but one wherein there is mutual respect for the individual branch responsibilities and their combined responsibilities to serve the country and its people.

I recommend that there be no term limits for the Office of the President and the Office of the Vice President. The present two-term limit should be eliminated and the question of a third term be left to the candidate and the voters.

I would also amend the Constitution so that the President and the Vice President are elected by popular voter rather than by the Electoral College. The Electoral College essentially votes each State's Delegates (total number of Representatives and Senators) based on the State's election results. The result is that a State like Alaska has three Delegates and California has 55 Delegates. In most cases, the State's winner wins all of the State's Delegates regardless of the how close the election results are. For this reason, a candidate with the highest popular vote can be defeated by a candidate that gets the majority of the Electoral College Delegates (this has actually happened). Note that I have recommended that the number of Representatives and Senators per State be drastically reduced so that the concept of the Electoral College (which is based on equal representation) would not apply. Please keep in mind that my recommendation has a significant advantage in that each vote is counted rather than the majority results of the election taking all of the State's votes as is the case for the Electoral College. I believe that this aspect of the Electoral College defeats the concept of equal representative as it denies that each vote be counted equally.

I would change the campaign financing laws similarly to those recommended for Representatives and Senators (refer to the section, "Fixing Federal Elections "). That is, campaign contributions allowed only by qualified registered voters. The amounts of contributions for individuals set at $1,000,000 per election and the candidates' own contribution limited to $1,000,000 per election, including personal loans to the campaign.

I would have only one Federal primary election with all qualified candidates from all parties on the ballot. The final election would include the top six winners of the primary election. Candidate statements would be provided to all voters together with a sample ballot. The ballots would not list party affiliation, although the candidate can include this in his/her statement. This is recommended so that voters do not blindly vote a strict one-party ballot. Note that this recommendation simplifies the present process of electing the President and the Vice President and provides wider choice of candidates to the voters.

The practice of States holding individual primary elections would be eliminated and would be replaced by the single Federal primary election. The elections would be decided by the popular vote totals. Also, voters would not be saddled with a limited choice between the two candidates put forward by the two dominate political parties. Let me emphasize this by stating that it is conceivable that the six candidates winning a place in the final election ballot could well be two each from the two dominant parties and two Independents. Clearly, this is a better choice than offered under the present system.

I would eliminate mid-term elections because they have been shown to be destructive in allowing good governance practices because of partisan politics.

My recommendations for Constitutional amendments include the election of the Attorney General who heads up the Justice Department and the Treasurer who heads up the Treasury Department. This would end the present practice of filling these positions with political appointees. My reasoning is that political appointees serve at the pleasure of the President and that that means their actions must align with those of the President.

I am not accusing any of our politically-appointed Treasurers or Attorney Generals of being political in carrying out their duties. However, I don't think it is a good idea to place these executives in important positions where they serve at the pleasure of the President.

It has not escaped my notice that the most serious problems that face our country have to do with these positions. I have pointed out that the Managing Trustee of the Social Security and Medicare programs is the Secretary of the Treasury. Clearly, the executives filling this position have failed their fiduciary duties, allowed bad accounting practices have mismanaged the programs and have remained silent to the false and misleading statements by the special interests. Also, these executives have allowed the country to reach a very serious position regarding Deficits and the Federal Debt. These executives could have sounded the alarm as I have done. However, they acted politically. I personally place partial blame of the foreclosure problem and the state of the economy on these executives.

I place the blame of the immigration problem with the executives filling the office of the Attorney General. Laws existed to prohibit illegal immigration. Yet these executives allowed the country to reach a very serious situation involving the millions of illegal immigrants residing in our country. Also, I have pointed out that not one of the Wall Street executives who violated the existing securities fraud laws and who were responsible for the foreclosure problem and the down economy has not been indicted.

I don't want readers to dwell on instances of bad actions; my purpose is to have voters support my recommendations to make these positions elected offices.

The Treasurer and Attorney General, being elected officials would come under the campaign financing law being recommended. Their salaries would be set at 80% of the

President's salary. The objective is to make the Treasurer and Attorney General independent of special interests and to attract top candidates.

The Treasurer and Attorney General would be elected in elections corresponding to Presidential elections and serve four-year terms. There would be no term limits. Candidates must be 36 years old or older at the time they take office and must be natural born citizens.

The Treasurer would recommend programs and budgets to Congress and the President to promote economic prosperity and financial security. Of course, the President would continue to submit his budget request to Congress. As is the present case, Congress would pass the budget in terms of appropriations. It is hoped that the reformed Congress would work with the other branches of the government to produce a good budget on schedule.

I would recommend that if Congress does not pass a balanced budget, the Treasurer will have the Constitutional authority to adjust the budget.

When the Federal Debt is over three times the forecasted Receipts, then the Treasurer can force that 10% of the Receipts are to be used to reduce the Debt. The Outlays approved by Congress will be reduced by the Treasurer by the required percentage to provide a balanced Budget. Below is an example for the 2014 Budget Actuals.

Actuals:

Receipts (without Social Security and Medicare)	$2.0 trillion
Outlays (without Social Security and Medicare)	2.6 Deficit
Adjusted per Treasurer:	0.6
Reduction in Federal Debt	$0.2 trillion
Remaining Receipts	1.8
Allowed Outlays	1.8
Deficit (Balanced Budget)	0.0

The reduction in Outlays necessary is 30.7%. At this point, Congress could submit a new budget and the process would continue to reach an agreement. However, at the start of the Fiscal Year, the Budget by the Treasurer would be the approved budget and Congress would be forced to accept the Reduction required at that instant.

I have deleted Social Security and Medicare because these programs are recommended to be off-budget items.

In my other articles, I have recommended ways to increase Receipts, reduce Outlays and thus reduce Actual Deficits. In summary, this reduces the Reduction necessary to achieve a Balanced Budget.

The Treasurer's budget will be the national budget unless Congress vetoes it with a vote of 75%, or greater. If vetoed, Congress will have to submit a budget which the Treasurer can adjust if not within the deficit limit. This process is continued to finalization. If the budget is not finalized by the start of the Fiscal year, the budget put forward by the Treasurer before the start of the Fiscal Year would become the Federal Budget. I recommend this process because I have witnessed the debacle in agreeing on the budget and to have approved budgets in time for the upcoming Fiscal year. In fact, for the year 2010-2011, Congress failed to appropriate funds in time for the start of the Fiscal year starting in October 1, 2010, and this was not accomplished until it was late by six months. And it was passed with the threat of shutting down the government.

Note that I am not changing our Constitution in regards that Congress is the only one that can approve spending and taxation. I am only allowing the Treasurer to reduce spending if he decides changes are required from that authorized by Congress. Note that I am not giving the Treasurer the authority to change the laws passed by Congress and signed by the President. I have recommended that laws be passed by Congress, with 75% votes, in the House and the Senate and signed by the President. I am only recommending that the Treasurer be allowed to decide how the limited income of the government is to be spent. The Treasurer would not be allowed to adjust the Tax Rates for individuals or corporations. Hopefully, when our Congress is reformed and starts acting responsibly, the actions of the Treasurer will be to agree with the Congress and the President with cooperative actions for the welfare of the country and its people. I was driven to this recommendation because we may not be able at first to completely eliminate partisan politics. It was for this reason that I did not want to recommend that the President be given line item veto. As political parties battle to control the Presidency and the House and Senate, I felt that it was best to have a fourth party (the Treasurer) to hopefully be independent of this battle for power. I recognize that political parties will also seek control of the Treasurer's office, but this ups the ante to achieve control of all four positions of power. Hopefully, the electorate will elect a Treasurer that can provide the independence required. In addition, keep in mind that the 75% votes by both houses of Congress eliminate partisan politics from this process.

In order to close loopholes, legislation during the Fiscal year could not exceed the national budget unless any new spending passed by Congress and signed by the President is approved by the Treasurer. This would take care of emergencies.

It is believed that these changes will bring our budgets to what are required to achieve the surpluses necessary to pay off our Federal Debt over a number of years.

With the results of polling of all qualified registered voters on issues, it is hoped that the will of the people will dominate in these difficult budget decisions.

I would prohibit the Treasurer from taking action to include spending on a new program or to take action to include new taxes. This is in keeping with my objective to leave these actions to Congress as called for in our Constitution. Please note that the authority of the Treasurer is null and void if the Congress passes a budget that meets fiscal responsibility to achieve the required goal set.

Keep in mind that the proposed approach allows Congress to avoid action by the Treasurer by passing budget authorizations within the zero-deficit limit; including interest due and an amount that reduces the Debt. Also consider that the deficit limit is what is required to pay for the Federal government expenditures while paying down our Federal Debt. I am against Balanced Budget or Zero Debt Constitutional Amendments.

My recommendations will remove the arguments about the debt limit. It is not responsible governance to continuously increase the debt limit. In my recommendations the debt is gradually reduced. At some point, we will be satisfied with a low Debt and proceed with a Debt Ceiling. Therefore, we can look forward to a combination of reduced taxes or increased spending while holding a Debt Ceiling.

The Treasurer will be required by the Constitution to provide quarterly and annual reports on the Federal Deficit and the Federal Debt and annual projections of these amounts for twenty years into the future. The Treasurer will be required to utilize standard accounting procedures including reporting Gross interest in the Federal Budget and borrowing in the Federal Debt for special securities sold to the Trust Funds. Interest to Trust Funds are not a gain to the government, therefore they need to be reported as expenditures. The same situation holds for special securities held by Trust Funds, they are a debt of the government. The government should not be allowed to satisfy interest due with an IOU to the Trust Funds and with the IOU used as a way to borrow additional funds and not include this debt in the Federal Debt.

The objective would be to provide citizens with an accurate accounting of the financial condition of the country. Apart from this, the Trustees of the Trust funds would be required to provide similar reports to the public. No longer will our elected officials and their political appointees be allowed to neglect the obligation they have to the economic prosperity and the financial security of the country and its people by misleading or incomplete reporting of financial issues.

I believe that the CBO should be moved to the Office of the Treasurer. The CBO accomplishes an important role in evaluating the financial impact of proposed legislation and transferring it to the Treasury would improve cooperation between the Treasurer's Office, Congress and the Executive Branch by having an independent Budget Office. This move would therefore ensure that politics would not enter into financial evaluations, thus protecting the country and its people.

The same argument as above could be made for moving the Office of Management and Budget from the Executive Branch to the Treasurer's Office. The same is recommended for the Council of Economic Advisors. I believe that if Congress and the Executive Branch have respect for the Treasurer's Office and establish a good working relationship, that this could be a big help in fixing the financial affairs of our country. Hopefully when we fix our broken government, we will find more ways to streamline our governmental functions and increase productivity of our government to provide essential Federal services at reduced cost.

Note that many States elect their Treasurer and Attorney General for the same reasons I make. I am confident that Americans will elect candidates who are well qualified for these important positions.

I would allow the President, as head of the Executive Branch, the Treasurer, as the head of the Treasury Department, and the Attorney General, as head of the Department of Justice, to make appointments of their staffs without the Congressional confirmation process. I make this recommendation because the confirmation process has become a very destructive force of partisan politics.

The Attorney General, which is a politically appointed position, is charged with enforcing the laws of the Federal government. This responsibly needs to be independent of the Executive Branch and special interests.

I would hope that with the election of the Attorney General that violators of our Federal laws would be vigorously pursued equally for all. Unfortunately, I don't agree that the Federal government is now dispensing justice equally to all Americans. Also, I am concerned that there are many violators of Federal law and I wonder if this is due to the fact that violators take a chance to break the law because they feel they can get away with doing so because the Federal government is not aggressive enough or if they feel they are protected as special interests. My objective is that violators will be deterred because they know that the Federal government is being very aggressive and that all violators will be in jeopardy. There is nothing more destructive to our democratic government and its people as corruption in our government and the violation of Federal laws. If we are to achieve greatness as a free society, we need to have all Americans be law abiding citizens and that justice for all is practiced equally.

Since the mission of the Office of the Solicitor General, part of the Department of Justice, is to represent the interest of the United States before the Supreme Court and to oversee appellate and certain other litigation on behalf of the United States in the lower Federal and State courts, I believe making the Attorney General independent of political ties will help strengthen equal justice for all and provide a check and balance to the rulings of the Supreme Court.

I find it unconscionable that private organizations are suing those associated with the fraudulent subprime loans, yet the Attorney General has not taken action at the Federal level to indict violators. Special interests want us to believe that applicable laws do not exist in these clear instances of securities fraud. Also, I find it unconscionable that we have a serious illegal immigration problem whose basis is the initial lack of law enforcement to eliminate entry into our country and deportation of the violators. The problem has been allowed to reach such proportions that it is now beyond solution.

The following additional reform should be considered. This is not an issue dealing with a broken government as my other recommendations have been. This is an issue to be considered because changes would correct a problem in our Constitution that could become significant in the future if we don't prepare for the consequences. In my previous recommendations, I have made specific recommendations. In this case, I ask that consideration be given to this recommendation because the arguments are not totally conclusive. There are questions involving whether the President and Vice President should be of the same political party, have the same opinions and have strong loyalties to each other. On the other hand, having a Vice President who is qualified to become President should have overwhelming consideration.

The Vice President is now nominated by the President and the Executive Branch is entirely filled with political appointees of the President. This brings up the issue whether an independent Vice President can provide needed checks and balances within the Executive

Branch now only provided by partisan politics. Then there are issues involving the line of succession to the Office of the President.

Let's pause here to discuss briefly the history of the Office of the Vice President. Clearly, the Constitution established the Office of the Vice President to provide a successor in the event of the President's death.

Fourteen of the former Vice Presidents have become President - more than half of them after the President had died. Since the 45th President is now serving, these figures are significant.

Our Constitution originally had the Office of the Vice President filled by the presidential candidate receiving the second highest Electoral College votes. This was implemented by the Electoral College members voting for two persons, one at least not an inhabitant of the same state as themselves. In 1800, there was a tie which was settled by the House of Representatives after thirty-five ballots. Because of this, Congress and the States passed the Twelfth Amendment to the Constitution instituting the present system wherein members of the Electoral College vote separate ballots for President and Vice President.

In 1792, Congress adopted the Presidential Succession Act providing that if a President died when there was no Vice President, the Senate President Pro Tempore and the Speaker of the House of Representatives, in that order, would succeed to the Office of the President. The Senate President Pro Tempore is a position voted in by the members of the Senate and is presently considered as the second most powerful position in the Senate, after that of the Vice President who is the President of the Senate. This position is different than the Majority Leader of the Senate. In 1886, Congress altered the line of succession to substitute cabinet members, in order of rank, for the congressional offices. In 1947, after the office of the Vice President had been vacant for most of a presidential term, Congress again changed the line of succession, naming the House Speaker as the next in line, followed by the Senate President Pro Tempore. Note that while this succession was a Constitutional issue, that Congress changed this by a Congressional law.
This was not right because it was not the proper way to change the Constitution.

In 1967, the Twenty-fifth Amendment was passed, stating that the President may appoint a Vice President to fill a vacancy in that office, subject to the approval by both houses of Congress. This was relied upon to replace Vice President Spiro Agnew when he resigned and to replace Vice President Gerald Ford when he replaced President Richard M. Nixon when he resigned. This Amendment also sets forth very specifically the steps that would permit the Vice President to serve as Acting President if a President is unable to discharge the powers and duties of the office.

As we discuss below, there are still significant issues involving the Office of the Vice President that need addressing. Let me make it clear that these issues are best addressed via a Constitutional Amendment which can only be passed by the people, rather than by being addressed by a broken government.

I recommend that Americans consider a Constitutional Amendment encompassing the following:

1. Stop the practice of the Vice-Presidential candidates being nominated by the Presidential nominee of each party. This is not to prohibit a Presidential nominee endorsing a preferred Vice-Presidential candidate.

2. Implement a separate election campaign for the Office of the Vice President.

3. The Vice President's salary will be 80% of the President's salary. The qualifications for the Vice president shall be the same as for the President.

4. The office of the Majority Leader of the Senate shall be eliminated and substituted for by the Senate President, elected by its members.

5. The present function of the Vice President to be President of the Senate shall be eliminated. With a 75% vote required to pass legislation the tie-breaking power of the Vice President is no longer required.

6. The functions of the Office of the Vice President are to carry out the remaining term of the President if and when the President is unavailable to serve or to serve temporarily as Acting President if the President is unable to discharge the powers and duties of office.

7. Recognizing that the Vice President can be called to fulfill the President's function on an instant's notice and perhaps during a national crisis, the Vice President has to be prepared. He should be familiar with all aspects of the Executive Branch, the other branches of the government, and knowledgeable with foreign leaders. This requires that he attends all cabinet meetings and national security briefings and meetings. There should not have to be a learning experience for the Vice President to function as required. These rights shall be written into the Constitutional Amendment. I do not like the aspect of the Twenty-fifth Amendment that allows the President to pick a Vice President even if approved by both houses of Congress because it does not yield a Vice Presidential candidate elected by the people. Instead, I would allow the President to appoint a Federally-elected officer and allow the appointee to serve without requiring Congressional approval. Such appointee could be a member of the House in Congress, a Senator, the Treasurer, the Attorney General, or a Justice of the Supreme Court. The Vice President would be sworn into office on the same day, just after the President is sworn into office, during a transition. I would allow the President and the Vice President to come to a mutual agreement to allow the Vice President to head up an initiative of the Executive Branch, such as making Americans the healthiest in the world.

8. The old procedure, that the second in line to the Presidency is the Speaker of the House, is not recommended because the officer may be ill- prepared to take over the President's office simply because he/she does not have the knowledge necessary as demanded above for the Vice President. Therefore, I would not use this procedure.

Note that my recommendation simply makes it a certainty that the offices of the President and the Vice President will always be filled with candidates that can be expected to perform the duties of these offices as required.

It is clear that voters for candidates to the Office of the Vice President will concentrate on the candidate's qualifications to assume the President's office. In a way, I am recommending a situation closely to how the Constitution was originally written; that is, that the Vice President is one that gets the votes to replace the President.

10. The Vice President should be able to speak out independently on national issues as an elected official of the people. This provides a check and balance of the Executive Branch now not available except via partisan politics. After all, the Vice president would want to have a healthy government to run if and when he might assume the Office of the President. Also, the Vice President would want to conduct himself so that he would be a popular candidate to someday run for the higher office of the President. The country would be the winner if such an experienced, popular and well-regarded figure became President.

I recognize that the above ideas can be a blessing or a disaster depending on whether both the President and Vice President are good responsible public servants (and why shouldn't these types be elected?).

Please note that I prefer that our President be an excellent executive as I consider his most important responsibilities to be to run our large Executive Branch. This should not prevent him from advocating for good governance, indeed this should be one of his responsibilities. Clearly, I demand adherence to the Constitution so that Congress passes the laws, sets taxes and passes appropriations to spend revenue. If we are to eliminate the bad aspects of partisan politics, we need to stop our President advocating as leader of his political party. He has been elected to the office to serve the people and the country and his responsibility is to make sure that the Executive Branch is run as efficiently as possible per the laws of the land. Let me make it clear that it is important that the President is seen as the leader of our country because that is what being Chief Executive Officer is all about.

Most of all, I want a government that works and one that works together amongst the three branches of our government to give us the best government the world will ever see. This requires government of the people, by the people and for the people and recognition that the people have a right and responsibility for good governance as stated in our Constitution.

Please note that in my opinion, Congress was wrong in passing the Presidential Succession Act. Such an issue is clearly a Constitutional issue and should be dealt with as such. When I discuss fixing the Supreme Court, I make recommendations to avoid this and similar violations in the future.

I recommend that the American people consider a Constitutional Amendment that consolidates ten Departments of the Executive Branch into three organizations, each headed by an elected official. The idea is to achieve improved operations and lower cost. Below is the recommended consolidation.

Executive Administrator	Executive Administrator	Executive Administrator
*Agriculture	*Education	* Energy
*Commerce	*Health and Human	* Interior
*Labor	Resources	* Transportation
Respective	*Housing and Urban	Respective
Employees	Development	Employees
100,000/		100,000/
38,000/	*Veteran's Affairs	70,000/
15,000	Respective	55,000
	Employees	
	4,200/65,000/	
	9,000/235,000	

President	Vice President
*Defense	
*Homeland Security	
*State	
*Executive Office	

There are many, many Boards, Commissions, Committees and Agencies in the Executive Branch. Some are part of Departments and this should remain. Those not assigned to Departments should be under the management of Executive Administrators in order that they can be properly managed. An effort should be made to validate the existence of these organizations and that they are necessary and provide a required function at reasonable cost. The fact is that the large Executive Branch does not now have the required function of management. Hopefully, the election of the Executive Administrators will provide this needed management function.

Note that the concept of the President's Cabinet would be eliminated. This would not prevent the President meeting with the three Executive Administrators to discuss issues and/or recommendations.

8. FIXING FEDERAL ELECTIONS

Our Founding Fathers were reluctant to have the election of the President settled by a popular vote. Of the two favorites (decided by votes of the States' Legislatures or decided by votes of the Electoral College), the latter was included in the Constitution. Fast forward to today when women are allowed to vote and when former slaves and their decedents are allowed to vote, we have an outdated Electoral College. Each State has Electoral votes equal to their number of Representatives and Senators and D. C. has three Electoral College votes. Because of the Political Parties dominance in each State, only about a dozen States are seen as Swing or Battleground States (wherein the parties fight to gain a majority of Electoral votes that decide the election). States, except Nebraska and Maine, vote their winner-take-all Electoral votes to the candidate with the highest popular vote. Unfortunately, this allows a candidate with a higher popular vote to lose the election based on Electoral votes (and this has happened).

I recommend eliminating the Electoral College and having the election winner decided by popular vote. I recommend elections every four years with a single national Primary and a General election. The six candidates with the highest popular votes in the Primary proceed to the General election. This would apply to the President and the Vice President. I recommend that the elections be conducted by the people and their elected government, not by the political parties.

As always, I want the Constitutional amendments and the laws written by the law schools and I want that there be national debates by the college debating societies.

Readers will note that the political parties will be against these changes because it deprives them of holding power and will help the people to regain their power of the vote.

I strongly believe that our broken government is also largely due to our campaign financing laws and partisan politics.

While we would all expect that our elected officials would be diligent in serving their constituents, independent of party membership or large campaign contributors, we must realize that loyalty to party and loyalty to those that contribute heavily to their campaign financing are very powerful forces that determine their actions in the final analysis because their election opponents do it and it is legal. I do not blame the good Representatives or Senators we elect, so much as the system we put them in. On the other side of the coin, these situations are not going to change, but only get worse, if we don't change the system and continue to vote for good candidates. And let's not fire our good elected officials, let's only fire those that we feel have violated the trust we have placed in them. You can identify those to fire by evaluating how they practice the bad aspects of partisan politics and how they support issues important to special interests rather than to Main Street. Don't just listen to their words, but evaluate their actions.

I am particularly concerned with the recent Supreme Court decision that allows Corporations and Unions to spend whatever they want on elections without limits as this will result in our elected officials fighting for these large contributions. The reasoning given by the Supreme Court that this was a question of free speech is unconscionable. Corporations can spend to support issues as a free speech right, but they don't have the right to contribute to the campaigns of candidates they feel will support their interests as the latter is not a free speech issue.

Let me start with what the Constitution says about elections. Only qualified registered voters within a District (for Representatives) and within the State (for Senators) can vote. In other words, this limited population alone gets to elect their Representatives and Senators to Congress. I would think that the Supreme Court would have held on to this right and prevented outsiders (of the District or State) to spend heavily on elections to select candidates that they might consider as sympathetic to their self-interests, especially if they could make large contributions to the campaigns of these individuals. The Supreme Court should have insisted that the elected officials serve their constituents and prohibited them from serving outside interests.

I don't know about you, but I am disgusted with the misleading and character assassination type TV ads. Unfortunately, they are effective and that is why they are used. Unfortunately, the media does not tell the people the truth about the information contained in these ads. The more money one has to sponsor these ads, the more effectiveness is gained because the voters are left confused and the less proper attention is given to sorting all this out and voting for the best candidate of the voters' self-interest.

As the saying goes, if you repeat a lie often enough, it becomes the truth. I would restrict Corporations and Unions, and all others that are not qualified registered voters, to spend what they want on issues (but not on candidates) and to be required to identify themselves on their endorsement on these issues, and not provide cash directly or indirectly to candidates' campaigns (as this can be interpreted as seeking favors).

In my previous book, "Saving Social Security and Medicare: Fixing the Retirement and Health Care Crises", I recount how the insurance companies favored the Republicans with their campaign financing and lobbying efforts to help them get control of Congress so that they could get the Medicare Private Insurance Plans passed (Parts C and D). Then they favored the Democratic Party to get the Health Care Reform legislation passed. After that, they starting favoring the Republican Party again to get the items in the Health Care Reform legislation that they were not happy with deleted. Clearly, special interests can be very successful in our present situation with campaign financing laws and partisan politics. Now with the Supreme Court decision to allow Corporations and Unions to spend whatever they want on elections the situation will only get worse.

If you think about this issue, I am certain that you will conclude that it is unfair (for say Corporations in Illinois) to spend whatever they want in specific Districts to elect District Representative candidates they feel will be sympathetic to their interests. If a candidate receives this level of support, he can't help but being sympathetic to the interests of these Corporations. In fact, this is one of the current problems with our broken government. Further, Americans are aware that if Corporations spend enough money with media exposure (without adequately revealing their sponsorship or motives) that these Corporations can affect the results of elections. That is why it is unfair for Americans in these Districts to lose their right to be fairly represented in Congress. Shame on the Supreme Court for their decision that allows Corporations and Unions to spend whatever they want on elections without limits. Note that I am for protecting the right of free speech even though campaign ads often include statements that are not defensible and violate good taste and values of fair competition.

Note that my recommendations result in Americans in Districts, State or Country to be better represented than they are now and which they will have in the future under the

Supreme Court ruling. Readers should take this into account when I recommend reducing the number of Representatives and Senators in Congress.

Now let us look at the issue of free speech. I am 100% for free speech for everyone, with limits. For example, we all know that it has been ruled that a person cannot holler "Fire" in a crowded room, if he knows that there is no fire and if there is a possibility of subsequent injury or death as the attendees stampede from the room. The idea is that one cannot tell a lie if he knows it is a lie and if the promotion of the lie could cause injury to others. I fault the Supreme Court for a decision without limits. Part of the problem is that the Supreme Court makes decisions on a thin 5 -to- 4 vote as was the case in this ruling. Below, I will provide my recommendations for limitations on campaign financing and freedom of speech as it pertains to elections.

In order to resolve these issues, we need to reform our campaign financing laws and make our elected officials financially independent so that they will not have to compete for large campaign contributions. At the same time, we need to place limitations on contributions so that we don't end up in the same place with candidates and elected officials fighting for large contributions and Corporations and Unions making large contributions to those that they believe will be sympathetic to their cause.

Also, we need to eliminate the bad aspects of partisan politics which is crippling the government's ability to work together to solve our country's problems.

In order to keep Representatives and Senators in Congress financially independent, I would increase their salaries to 65% and 80%, respectively, of that of the President's salary. Later, I will provide recommendations to reduce the membership of Congress because it has gotten too large an organization to assign responsibility. In this regard, let me state that the media does not report to me how my Representative voted (this is somewhat understandable because California has 53 Representatives).

I would not have term limits so that a candidate could hopefully look forward to a long career if constituents were supportive of their efforts and kept re-electing them.

Then there is the issue of loyalty to a political party that transcends loyalty to country, loyalty to constituents and loyalty to accepted values being replaced by loyalty to a political party solely for political reasons. While no Representative or Senator will claim this exists on their or their party's part, I believe that Americans see thru all of this and form their opinion on instances wherein this becomes an issue. Keep in mind that loyalty to a political party is a powerful force that cannot be easily ignored. If this is violated in today's political climate, a candidate or elected official is ruining his chances of being elected or re-elected and is an action that dooms his political career.

I want Americans to realize that political parties do not provide advantages to citizens as much as they serve the interests of the parties themselves. The proof is that both political parties have failed and continue to fail the American people. Political parties are organized to select their candidates and have them elected. This is the way they derive and hold onto political power. Political parties select the candidates they want to sponsor and they solicit voters to vote for their elected candidates based on party. I would like for Americans to encourage the best candidates to run for office and to vote for the best candidates that support voter demands, irrespective of party. However, I realize that this Utopia will be difficult to achieve even though I believe that this is what our founding fathers had in mind when establishing our democracy. This is why I recommended that only qualified registered voters be allowed to make campaign contributions to candidates.

Below are specific recommendations on campaign financing:

1. Only qualified registered voters in their Districts (for Representatives) or their State (for Senators) and the country (for national Federal offices) could make contributions to candidates and elected officials. Voters will have to be satisfied by candidates in order for candidates to receive campaign contributions.

2. The maximum contribution would be $1,000,000 per qualified registered voter per election. This contribution must come from the voter's own assets. The giving of a

contribution to a voter in order that the voter can use it to make his contribution would be prohibited (and punishable by a severe penalty).

3. Corporations, Unions, PAC's, Political Parties, the government and all others (except qualified registered voters as stated in 1 above) would be prohibited from making contributions to candidates and elected officials. However, they would be allowed to promote their special interests' issues (but not support or contribute to candidates directly or indirectly). Candidates can take sides on issues in vying for votes and thus provide voters with arguments on both sides of issues. These arguments are now not available to the voting public because the special interests are mostly the only ones spending heavily on media exposure to get their side of an issue accepted with little competition. No longer will candidates be surrogates of the special interests. No longer will special interests be allowed to sway public opinion on candidates to steer votes to their choices. This would close the present loophole allowing foreign contributions being made indirectly through stateside organizations. There would be severe penalties for violators.

4. Candidates could contribute up to $1,000,000 to their own campaigns per election. This limit is set to increase the pool of possible top candidates and to avoid a candidate to buy an election. This contribution must come from the candidates own assets. The giving of a contribution to a candidate in order that the candidate can use it to make his contribution would be prohibited. There would be severe penalties for violators. The $1,000,000 limit would include personal loans made to the campaign fund.

5. Campaign contributions could only be spent to support election campaigns.

6. Campaign contributions left over from an election would have to be rolled over to the next election. This would not affect contribution limitations for the next election. Candidates would be allowed at this time to withdraw the amount (or a portion thereof) of their loan for the last campaign, provided funds were available from the left-over contributions. The amounts due from the candidate for loans would carry forward until paid off in full.

7. If a candidate or elected official stops running for election or re-election at the next election, unused campaign contributions would have to be donated to a charitable organization of their choosing provided the organization does not benefit the candidate or elected official or their families.

The following additional reforms are recommended:

1. Four-year terms for Representatives and Senators

2. Elections corresponding to Presidential elections. We are recommending eliminating midterm elections. This saves some money. Also, it is hoped that this will eliminate some bad aspects of partisan politics which has been the emphasis for mid-term elections.

3. The Election Commission to publish Candidates' statements for use by the voters. This would be mailed together with a sample ballot to all qualified registered voters at least two months before the election.

4. The ballots would not list the party affiliation. However, the candidate could include this in his statement. Sample ballots would be sent out together with the candidates' statements in 3 above. This is to be done to prevent voters voting a strict party ballot without regard to the candidates' qualifications and statement.

5. Primary elections would include all qualified candidates from all political parties and all others not affiliated with a political party. There needs to be a set of rules to be met to become a qualified candidate.

6. The top six winners of the primary election would be included in the final election ballot. Note that the voter could have a choice of more than one candidate from a political party.

7. Citizens registering to vote would have to provide proof of qualification to vote. I have included this because I fear that the existing process can register voters that are not qualified to vote. Keep in mind that this is meant to be a once in a lifetime ordeal.

8. Federal rules for elections would be set to insure fair and accurate elections and to provide the possibility of a recount being required.

9. Severe penalties would be imposed for violation of election laws by voters, candidates and others.

10. Elected officials and their families would be prohibited from receiving anything of value from anyone. This is a very tough law, but it very necessary to keep our elected officials independent of special interests and eliminating any basis for conflict of interest.

11. The media and others would be required to provide equal and like coverage to all candidates for a particular office. If there are sponsored election related events, this means that all qualified candidates for a particular office will be given equal and like coverage. I recognize that this limits what events can be conducted, but it is absolutely necessary to be fair to all candidates. A format that would be to the voters' interest would be to allow all candidates to make a statement and for the moderator to ask the same questions to each of the candidates. The questions could be solicited from the constituents.

12. While I don't have a recommendation to avoid misleading or character assassination ads typically run on the media by candidates, I would hope that the voters will be smart enough not to be swayed by such ads. Also, I hope that voters will reject irresponsible candidates that succumb to bad practices. This is not meant to eliminate ads that distinguish between candidates. However, I recognize that it's a matter of personal interpretation whether the ad is meaningful or not.

13. Political ads would be required to clearly state the organizations sponsoring the ad (making up 75% of the cost of the campaign), state the cost of the ad campaign and state the approval of the organizations sponsoring the ad. These statements are required to be visible and spoken and not be subjected to fine print or instant nonreadable exposure.

14. The government would be prohibited from funding candidates' campaigns. This would prohibit elected or appointed officials from using government paid travel, time,

etc. to support a candidate. This would not prohibit elected or appointed officials from endorsing a candidate.

15. I haven't completely figured out how Americans can effectively voice their positions on issues, but I think this would be beneficial to elections and to the actions of our government. If "American Idol" can process 60 million votes in a few hours, there must be a way of getting this done. This polling would not be an official position, but only an accurate polling of how those polled voted. One problem that needs to be given attention to is making sure that each position on issues is valid and that the results are presented accurately and fairly. A start in this direction would involve providing each qualified registered voter a confidential ID identifying the voter, his District and State.

Keep in mind that at this point, we are only talking about two offices (Representative and Senator). Since we are recommending these elections corresponding to Presidential elections every four years, we can add two more offices (President and Vice President). We have recommended that two Supreme Court Justices be elected in each election until nine elected Justices were seated on the Court. This brings the total offices on the ballot to six. Later, when we discuss Fixing the Executive Branch, we will recommend two more offices (Attorney General and Treasurer) to be included in Federal elections for a total of eight. In addition, we will recommend three more offices (three Executive Administrators) for a total of eleven. Certainly, the ballot will not be overwhelming at the Federal level. It is hoped that this recommended ballot will attract more voters and provide coverage to all candidates for all offices. Because of the recommended campaign financing recommendations, we should be spared the high volume of TV ads dealing with elections.

Voters need to realize that their votes are local for Senators and Representatives. Voters should vote for the Senators and Representatives they are confident will meet their individual (voters') demands, that are qualified and trustworthy, and that do not practice the bad aspects of partisan politics. Voters should guard against being confused by political parties and special interests that put forth other reasons for voters to vote their local situation.

Below is data on the Presidential elections of 2004 and 2008.

	2004	2008
% Voting Age Voted	55	58
% Votes for Demo/Repub	99	98
% Margin of Winner Votes Over Next Candidate	5	16

The primaries fuel the bad aspects of partisan politics because the issue is about which political party will rule the day. As the primary elections and caucuses occur over time, totals for delegates for each candidate for the convention and total Electoral College votes for each candidate are tracked and advertised (which can influence voters yet to vote).

The present system of primary elections and the final election process is not a good way to place the power of the vote in the hands of the American people. It is a system wherein essentially the winner in each State can win all Delegates to the convention and to the Electoral College. This creates a problem that the candidate with the highest popular vote can lose the election. I have recommended a single primary before the final election with each vote treated equally, see above.

I was very disappointed in the 2016 Presidential primary elections that the media did not make it clear that the parties had rules that prevented all registered voters from voting for their choice regardless of the party of the voter or the party of the candidate and that the delegates won by the winners were not based on the popular vote.

Americans must recognize that our political system for elections does not meet the criteria for a Democracy.

As always, I recommend that national debates be held by college debating societies and that laws and Constitutional Amendments be written by law schools.

9. FIXING PARTISAN POLITICS

If we are to fix the bad aspects of partisan politics, we need to recognize that there are strong forces that cause this problem and that must be dealt with if we are to resolve it.

One force is campaign financing. We have taken care of that in the article "Fixing Federal Elections". The other force is political power which we treat below.

Political power results from receiving large campaign contributions because the party in power has the votes to pass any legislation the party is asked to pass by the special interests. Political power also results in the party being able to Chair all Committees, the Speaker of the House and the Majority Leader of the Senate. These advantages derive to the political party as well as to its members. Therefore, loyalty to party is demanded.

The above is why a political party punishes a member that sides with the arguments of the other party, who votes with the other party or who states concern about his/her's own partity's stand on an issue. We cannot solve partisan politics unless we get to the point where members of political parties have respect for other members of Congress regardless of party. After all, members have different constituents who might have different needs. I think our founding fathers recognized this and tried to establish a representative House and Senate that would establish a debating forum in order to reach a consensus on what is the best for all the people and the country. We don't need everyone to agree, we only need to hear all arguments and come to a majority decision. Some decisions now require a simple majority (51%), others take a 60% majority and passing of Constitutional amendments to be ratified by the States Legislatures takes a 75% majority (38 States out of 50 States). I have always felt that I would be most happy with requiring a 75% vote for Congress (the House or the Senate) to pass legislation as that would signify a consensus. On the other hand, I believe that the 51% and 60% votes fuel the bad aspects of partisan politics because they demand a party to seek these majorities to establish their power to carry a vote. Also, I believe that the 51% and 60% votes allow bad legislation to be passed when a party has the required power. On the other hand, a requirement for a 75% vote requires the parties to work together because no party will have a 75% majority.

It is inconceivable that a single party could achieve a majority of 75% as this would leave the other parties to share the remaining 25%. An advantage of the reduced size Congress recommended is that it would only take only 9 more votes in the House (44 versus 35) and 8 more votes in the Senate (38 versus 30) to attain a 75% vote over a 60% vote. This appears possible if we are able to temper down partisan politics.

Just think if members of both parties would be for the passing of some good legislation and produce a 75% vote. This is what we need to achieve in the end for all our reforms. Presently, a party with a 60% majority can demand their legislation be passed and can decline to compromise. We witnessed this in the Debt Ceiling Increase compromise.

Unfortunately, there are some in Congress that value party loyalty above everything else, including country, constituents and established values. Voters need to identify them and vote to remove them from office as they are the villains of our broken government. Voters have a part to play in that some voters are party loyalists and therefore feed this problem. That is why we witness a political party acting and voting as a block.

I am not against political parties as they represent a very important role in checks and balances and preventing abuse of power. They also help in bringing power to the bargaining table; however, this can be a bad aspect.

Just think of what we would have if we had only one dominate political party. As we are witnessing, it is not beneficial to have two dominant parties that hold the country divided equally as that creates grid-lock as we have the worst situation with the bad aspects of partisan politics. My opinion is that we need more than two political parties with none being dominate (i.e., carrying a 75% vote capability). This would force the parties to work together to reach a consensus amongst parties. Therefore, we should not be hesitant to prevent a party from getting too powerful. Historically, for decades, we have been switching majority between the two dominant parties and this has only worsened the situation because we have created a strong force to seek and hold power. We need to have a Congress whose first and only priority is serving the country and the people. My writings should be of help to voters because I have made recommendations that we want Congress to take action on. If a voter accepts these recommendations, the voter needs to vote for those candidates that promise to act on these recommendations, regardless of party (assuming the candidate is qualified and trustworthy).

I believe a better alternative to a dominant political party is for small ad hoc groups of Representatives and/or Senators, irrespective of party affiliation, to band together to rally their associates to pass specific needed reform. This is the way a democratic Congress should work to serve the country and its people. I would be most happy if individual members of Congress, irrespective of party, started a petition to save Social Security and Medicare and bypassed party leaders, partisan politics and party loyalty. This would be a rebellion against the way they have been treated by party leaders who make deals in private meetings and force their party members to align themselves with a decision they have not had a chance to debate or influence.

In competitions, we are taught to perform to our best efforts, to respect other competitors and to congratulate the winner. Unfortunately, this concept is not the rule in Congress, because the competition is about power and campaign contributions. And the power and campaign contribution issues have nothing to do about serving the country and its people. It is about political power for the political party and its loyal members. Just contemplate on the many actions of Congress we have witnessed by dominate political parties that do not serve the country or the people, but only the special interests. And it is precisely this that we need to eliminate.

Let's make it clear that we want Congress to serve the country and their constituents, not the special interests. This is why I feel so strongly against the Supreme Court decision to let Corporations and Unions to spend whatever they want on elections, without limit. This will certainly increase the problem we face with partisan politics because there will be a partisan movement to seek and obtain these large campaign contributions. It also destroys the concept of giving representation in Congress to constituents of specific Congressional Districts and States. I can envision Wall Street corporations in the State of New York spending hundreds of millions of dollars in elections across the country to elect candidates who they feel will be sympathetic to their special interests. In this scenario, these corporations will be determining the outcome of elections. I say this, because the money spent on campaigns is a big force to have voters vote as the special interests would want.

I recognize that in reality, we will never be able to eliminate partisan politics or the rise of dominant political parties. However, we can temper the bad aspects of these situations in order to achieve a better working government.

I have made many recommendations that go a long way to resolving the partisan politics problem in the above section, "Fixing Federal Elections ". This is true because candidates and elected officials will now have to satisfy constituents to maximize campaign contributions instead of the special interests and this is way it should be.

Below are additional recommendations.

1.   Having the House and the Senate members vote for Speaker of the House, the Majority Leader of the Senate and Committee Chairs, regardless of political party. These elections would be by secret ballot to protect the voters. Hopefully, the best elected officials will receive the votes to win these important positions. The idea is that these positions will be filled with members that are trusted and respected by both parties to be fair to all. Hopefully, the Chairs will appoint committee members regardless of party. These Chairs should select members of their committees to represent all parties as equally as possible. At the present time, the dominate party rules, and this fuels partisan discontent.

2.   Americans deserve to hear all ideas and views instead of only two, one from each of the two dominate political party spokespersons, as this fuels partisan politics. I think Americans care more about a good idea for legislation rather than giving credit to a political party. Therefore, I would ask the media to report on these ideas by members of Congress without stressing political party affiliation. Another idea is for the media to refrain from reporting the statements of political party spokespersons on issues, but instead seeking out alternate views on the issues without stressing political party affiliation. Another idea is for the media to have positions supported so that Americans can hear the pros and cons associated with issues being debated (this is now lacking). And finally, it would be best if a group representing all parties proposed legislation and are interviewed by the media to discuss their legislation.

3.   The American people can play a very important part in eliminating partisan politics by voting for the best candidate, regardless of party affiliation. Also, Americans can help by resisting being partisan in their own actions. After all, no party or party member is perfect on every issue all of the time.

4.   I would eliminate the Congressional confirmation process for political appointees of the President, the Treasurer and the Attorney General. I recommend this because the confirmation process has become a very destructive force of partisan politics.

Let me admit that it will be very difficult to resolve partisan politics and it will take a long time to accomplish the changes necessary to meet this objective. But certainly, if we make the reforms recommended, this will go a long way to reach this objective. I would want that if Americans demanded the fixing of Social Security and Medicare, that Congress could support this regardless of political party. However, as we have witnessed for years, this issue goes unresolved, the problem gets worse and the window for resolution keeps closing. And note that we have not had a serious debate on these important issues. Perhaps the people have to support an initiative to be voted on to resolve these issues.

This brings up an important issue on national debates dealing with important issues needing resolution. It would very constructive for the country to witness debates on fixing the immigration problem which has resulted in 11 million illegal immigrants living in this country. A series of national debates would be helpful in arriving at a solution. What is needed is for someone to recommend a solution and then have national Debates For with Rebuttals and Against with Rebuttals. And this scenario could be repeated to arrive at a solution that has consensus of the people through the voter polling I have recommended.

As is my approach, I recommend that Law Schools take on the responsibility to write the Amendments and new laws and that national debates are held by college Debating Societies. I want the emerging leaders of our country (the young people) to participate in the resolution of the problems the country faces now and in the future.

Since Americans can only count on the Constitution to protect themselves and the country, I want the Constitution to be amended so that the rights are spelled out without question. If there is a problem resulting from partisan politics due to strong real forces that result in problems, I want this problem to be resolved now and for the future. We must not let partisan politics control. We must have safe guards to prevent partisan politics from affecting the welfare of the country and its people.

10. Fixing Federal Deficits and the Federal Debt

Federal spending in recent years has resulted in large Deficits and as a consequence, the Federal Debt has risen to high levels.

Sadly, our government has not done anything to correct these problems. In fact, they have caused the problems.

Clearly, there is a limit on how much Debt the country can carry. If the limit is exceeded, we run the risk that lenders will conclude that the borrowed funds, with interest, run the risk of not being paid back. In particular, China may redeem their investments and not renew them. In turn, this may force our government to have to pay higher interest rates to secure loans and/or not being able to secure the necessary loans at reasonable interest rates.

I would recommend that if Congress does not pass a balanced budget, the Treasurer would have the Constitutional authority to adjust the budget.

In the article, Fixing the Executive Branch, I recommend that the Treasurer be an elected official rather than an appointed official

When the Federal Debt is over three times the Receipts, then the Treasurer can force that 10% of the Receipts are to be used to reduce the Debt. The Outlays approved by Congress will be reduced by the Treasurer by the required percentage to provide a balanced Budget. Below is an example for the 2014 Budget Actuals.

Actuals:

Receipts (without Social Security and Medicare) *	$2.0 trillion
Outlays (without Social Security and Medicare) *	2.6
Deficit	0.6

Adjusted per Treasurer:

Reduction in Federal Debt	$0.2 trillion
Remaining Receipts	1.8
Allowed Outlays	1.8
Deficit (Balanced Budget)	0.0

*I have deleted Social Security and Medicare because these programs are recommended to be off-budget items. These programs would be made self-supporting.

The reduction necessary in Allowed Outlays is 30.7%. At this point, Congress would veto the above budget and would submit a new budget and the process would continue to reach an agreement. However, at the start of the Fiscal Year, the Budget by the Treasurer would be the approved budget and Congress would be forced to accept the Reduction required at that instant.

I will recommend ways to increase Receipts, reduce Outlays and thus reduce Actual Deficits. In summary, this reduces the Reduction necessary to achieve a Balanced Budget.

I have shown that Medicare can be saved with a reduction in spending of General Revenue totally $238 billion annually. That leaves $362 billion of the $0.6 trillion to be reduced. I show below how this can be achieved.

The Treasurer's adjusted budget will be the national budget unless Congress vetoes it with a vote of 75%, or greater. If vetoed, Congress will have to submit a budget that the Treasurer can adjust if not within the deficit limit. This process is continued to finalization. If the budget is not finalized by the start of the Fiscal year, the budget put forward by the Treasurer before the start of the Fiscal Year would become the Federal Budget. I recommend this process because I have witnessed the debacle in agreeing on the budget and to have approved budgets in time for the upcoming Fiscal year. In fact, for the year 2010-2011, Congress failed to appropriate funds in time for the start of the Fiscal year starting in October 1, 2010, and this was not accomplished until it was late by six months. In addition, it was passed with the threat of shutting down the government.

During and following the recent recession, the Federal Reserve printed money which was used to buy Treasuries. This action kept interest rates low for Treasuries and thus helped in a small way to reduce the increase in the Federal Debt. The interest earned was consequently transferred to the Treasury by the Federal Reserve, thus reducing, in a small way, the Deficit. Because the Federal Debt was growing, the government had to continue to increase the total amount it had to have as borrowed. The Federal Reserve finally stopped the buying of Treasuries as the economy improved slightly and as the necessity to keep interest rates low was reduced.

The United States is the world's premier marketplace. Companies all over the world desire to serve this market in order to increase their revenue and profit. If the country's economy is booming, this helps the market. Thus, Companies should recognize that it is good for their bottom line that Americans enjoy a low unemployment rate with good wages as this increases the value of the market place. Therefore, when special interests complain about the high-income tax rates for Corporations, they are ignoring that the marketplace deserves a high-income tax rate.

I recommend that tax credits for R&D expenditures and purchase of Capital Equipment be eliminated. These items are part of running a business and the company should not receive tax credits for these items. I also recommend that income tax rates be held high and that companies that do not pay their fair share of funding the country be prohibited from doing business in the country.

It is necessary that companies that move to other countries to avoid paying their fair share of running the country not to be allowed to conduct business in the country. In addition, companies should not be allowed to park their foreign profits to avoid paying income taxes on these profits.

In the early 1950's, corporate taxes accounted for 32% of General Revenue when the top rate was 52%. My proposal calls for a top rate of 35% as now exists. I calculate that corporate taxes will account for only 24% of General Revenue with my recommendations.

I believe that the required reduction of $362 billion discussed above to eliminate the entire Deficit of $0.6 trillion can be achieved from Corporate America and from the Hedge Fund and Wall Street organizations that enjoy an unfair reduction in income tax. Below is the recommended Budget

Reduction in Federal Debt	$0.2362 trillion
Receipts	
(With additional $362 billion) *	2.362
Spending	2.126
(With $238 billion reduction) **	
Deficit	0.0

* This is the increase discussed above

** This is the reduction discussed above

The $0.6 trillion reduction would be achieved as follows:

Savings on Medicare	$238 billion
Increase in taxes for Capital Spending Write-Offs	$150 billion
Increase in taxes for R&D tax credits	$100 billion
Increase in taxes for Hedge Fund Managers	$112 billion
And Wall Street*	
Total	$600 billion ($0.6 trillion)

As always, I recommend that the CBO provide their own independent figures for the recommendations above and bring them up to date. In addition, as always, I recommend a national debate by the collage debating societies and the writing of Constitutional Amendments by the Law Schools.

* It may necessary to reconsider the Estate Tax reduction and the Bush Tax Cut extension for all to reach this level of increased additional revenue necessary to balance the Budget as indicated here.

The Constitutional Amendment would include that the ceiling on the Federal Debt at the end of the Fiscal Year would be the Debt at the end of the previous Fiscal Year minus the above reduction in the Federal Debt.

The beauty of the recommended plan is that it succeeds in the first year and for many years into the future.

It is seen that fixing the Federal Deficits and the Federal Debt is relatively easy. All it takes is to Save Social Security and Medicare and to stop the give-a-ways given to Corporate America, the Hedge Fund Managers and Wall Street on a permanent basis.

Please consider boycotting the TV program "60 Minutes" until they find it in the people's interest to air an episode on this issue.

Let me make it clear that I am not for raising the corporate tax rate. I am only asking that corporations pay their fair share of operating our great country. I want to eliminate such giveaways as the $250 billion in tax credits provided in the Extension of the Bush Tax Cut Compromise. Keep in mind that there are many more examples that the wealthy, corporations, hedge fund partners, Wall Street and other special interests are given to reduce the amount they should fairly pay in taxes. Can one argue that it is not fair for corporations to retain only 65% of their pre-tax earnings?

Let us consider the 2010 compromise on extending the Bush Era tax cuts. Below is a summary of the compromise.

Total Cost, in Billions

	Individuals	Wealthy	Corporations Extending Bush
Tax Cuts	($383)		-
Capital Spending			
Write-offs	-	-	$150
Estate Tax Reduction	-	$88	-
Payroll Tax Reduction	($120)		-
Jobless Benefits	$56	-	-
Tax Credits for			
Families	($40)		-
R&D Tax Credits	-	-	$100
Subtotals	$56	$88	$250
	($543)		-
Total		$937	

These figures are expected to be greater than the above figures when brought up to date. Note that the law passed gave these give-a-ways for all years into the future guaranteeing trillion-dollar deficits for the future. In addition, this was on top of the poor economy due to the Great Depression of 2008-2009.

Loss of Revenue, in Billions

Subtotal $761*

Increase in Spending, in Billions

Subtotal $56 (for Jobless benefits)

Loss of Income to Social Security, in Billions

                                    $120 (reduction in Payroll Taxes)

Total $937

* Capital Equipment Spending Write Offs, Estate Tax Reduction, Tax Credits for Families, Extending Bush Tax Cuts and R&D Tax Credits.

I have made a case that in our situation we need to reduce spending and increase revenue. The compromise does just the opposite as it increases spending by $56 billion and reduces revenues by $761 billion for an increase in the deficit of $937 billion, including the $120 billion reduction in the Payroll Tax. I am against the Payroll Tax reduction unless the government would replace the funds lost to the Social Security Trust Fund (otherwise it is just another nail in the coffin of the program) and I understand this will be done (therefore this item should be included in the spending category). However, I suspect this will be accomplished via an IOU, which hurts the Social Security program as it makes its problem worse. Note that in the 75-year history of Social Security that government funding has been zero. Now that achievement will be lost, because critics will now be able to point out that in 2011, the government spent $120 billion on Social Security out of General Revenue (the critics will not confess that this was a payment for money owed).

The $250 billion tax credits for Corporations listed was not warranted because I have made a point that Corporations are not paying their fair share of operating the Federal government. In addition, I have made a case that these tax credits will not improve the unemployment problem or the economy and are just give-a-ways to special interests. I consider Capital Equipment purchases and R&D expenditures a part of accomplishing and continuing business operations. Therefore, I do not support these tax credits. I do agree that the government should sponsor things like cancer research when private industry has no business incentive to pursue them. In addition, I do agree to loans to create good paying, long-term jobs.

I agree with the spending of the $56 billion for extending jobless benefits.

I disagree on reducing the Payroll tax as a give-a-ways to Corporate America.

I disagree on cutting the Estate Tax further I agree on Tax Credits for Families.

None of the proposals in the compromise will reduce the unemployment problem or improve the economy and of course that was not the reason they were included in the compromise. I do support effective efforts to reduce the unemployment problem and to improve the economy.

I must discuss with my readers how I feel about the partisan legislation. What was agreed to was to provide significant not-necessary advantages to the wealthy and Corporations for modest short-term essential advantages provided to middle and low-income families (but with disastrous long-term problems with Deficits and the Federal Debt). I do not call this compromise. My argument is that compromise is where both sides agree to extend jobless benefits with one side wanting to extend them for one year and the other side wanting to extend them for only six months. The compromise would be to split the difference. In other words, the principle both sides agree to is to extend jobless benefits and the two sides agree to compromise by splitting the difference on the period of the extension. This is different than one side for and the other side against extending jobless benefits, but coming to agreement if large tax credits were given to Corporations. **Is there any question that the unemployed need jobless benefits more than GE need a giveaway?** In this latter instance, each party violated its principle and this is not what I call compromise. It is capitulation on both sides. I would rather know which party stood for extending jobless benefits and which party was against this on an individual vote. More important to individual Americans is how their Representatives and Senators voted on this important issue. I would want Americans to know the facts so they could decide on which party and candidates to vote for depending on their own judgment of the situation. I would want the government to delay action, have a national debate on the issue, poll all qualified registered voters and have Congress vote on the individual issue. This way the people would be able to assign responsibility to their Representatives and Senators in Congress representing their interests. **After all, in our democratic system it is the will of the people that counts, not the decision of political parties seeking to win the next election.** These were issues that have been neglected for some time and there was no real reason to wait to the last minute to act upon them. In addition, I am against Congress lumping many issues under a single legislation because the people's interests are preempted on individual issues.

In the case of the extension of the Bush Era tax cuts, I would have preferred that they were left to expire if a true compromise on this individual issue could not be reached, as this would have reduced the Deficit by $383 billion. The real issue was whether the tax cuts for the non-wealthy be extended and the tax cuts for the wealthy be eliminated. There was room to negotiate since the breakpoint for the non-wealthy and the wealthy was flexible. I would want a national debate, polling of all registered voters and a Congressional vote. In this way, Americans could assign responsibility to their Representatives and Senators and keep score on their performance. This is the democratic way of government of the people, by the people and for the people.

Clearly, one problem the country has is that Corporate America, the large banks, the large financial institutions and the large insurance and pharmaceutical companies have corrupted our government and are not acting as good members of our society. In addition, they are being allowed to continue to act in this way.

Do not allow our broken government to abolish the IRS or to reform our tax system in radical ways such as a flat tax. There is nothing wrong with the IRS nor our tax system except for the give-a-ways discussed above. Therefore, it is relatively easy to correct for the Federal Deficits and the Federal Debt as discussed above. What is needed is to fix our broken government so that it serves the people, not the special interests. I have provided numerous articles on how to fix our broken government.

11. Tax Reform

My plan for a tax cut for the low-income and middle-class reporting $250,000 maximum taxable income in 2017 (married, filing jointly) would reduce the tax due from $10,453 to $5,227 (a saving of $5,226) for filers reporting $75,900 taxable income or higher (up to the $250,000 cap).This to be accomplished simply by cutting the marginal tax rates for the two lowest brackets by half (from 10% to 5% and from 15% to 7.5%). The total tax reduction would cost $836 billion based on an estimated 160 million filers effected. Below we have identified $100 billion surplus that could be applied to this cost. We could pay for more of the cost by reducing the tax loopholes given to Wall Street and Hedge Fund Managers and to pass-through business owners and/or reducing the $250,000 cap to reduce the number of filers receiving the $5,226 tax cut.

Note how this $860 billion tax cut for the low-income and middle-class compares to the 2010 and 2017 $1,000 billion tax cuts for companies and the wealthy. This indicates that we could find the $736 Billion necessary from the $2,000 billion given to the companies and wealthy.

Also compare this to the campaigns by the special interests that call for a 70% marginal tax rate for income above $10 million. This the same tactic followed by the special interests to ensure keeping the status quo and diverting dialogue to distasteful ideas that avoid discussions of sound alternatives. We report this same tactic with Social Security and Medicare and with Healthcare ("Medicare for All").

My recommendation is that Americans support retaining and correcting our present tax system by deleting laws that allow Corporations not to pay any Federal Income Taxes on their huge profits and that allow wealthy individuals to avoid paying their fair share of Federal Income Taxes.

Our tax laws have been passed during decades of Congresses from both parties. I cannot believe that the majority of the laws were not well founded. Also, I will point out that a few of the laws were wrong and need correcting. Also, I will point out that the proposed tax reform by the GOP is very wrong as it provides give-a-ways to the wealthy while hurting the middle class and the poor. A simple case in point is the deletion of Medical Deductions. The current law allows deductions above 10% of the Adjusted Gross Income. Wealthy individuals cannot take these deductions because of the 10% clause. However, the middle class and the poor can reduce their taxes with the current law. Therefore, we need to correct what is wrong and prevent making changes that are wrong. Fortunately, this idea was dropped.

In the article on Fixing Federal Deficits and Federal Debt I discussed deleting the laws that provide tax credits for R&D Expenditures and for Capital Equipment purchases. These expenses are normal expenses of doing business. Corporations use these tax credits to avoid paying their fair share of Federal income taxes. In the article on tuition-free college education I discussed changing the Estate Tax law to fund twenty, or more, inner-city institutions providing tuition-free academic and vocational training. The corrected law would allow an inheritance of $3 million, Tax-free, with the remainder taxed as ordinary income. If the new Estate Tax would allow the first $3 million Tax-Free and the balance subject to be taxed as ordinary income, a $100 million Estate would yield $66.05 million after taxes with taxes of $36.95 million (35%).

There are other laws that allow the wealthy and other special interests to avoid paying their fair share of Federal Income Taxes and these loopholes should be corrected.

Our country has a progressive tax system that allows low-income individuals and corporations not to have to pay any Federal Income Taxes. Also, the system has seven tax brackets with increasing tax on increasing income until it reaches a maximum tax of approximately 35% for the very high-income individuals and corporations (this above a very high income of approximately $250,000). Ideas of a flat tax or other ideas are not progressive and do not correct the problems of the present system. Clearly, reducing the top tax rate from 35% to 15% for corporations and the wealthy is not a good idea for the people and the country. Also, I am leery about ideas to reduce Itemized Deductions in place of doubling the Standard deduction for individuals. I believe that this will increase taxes for many Americans who would be better off with the status quo.

In the early 1950's, corporate taxes accounted for 32% of General Revenue when the top tax rate was 52%. In 2009, corporations contributed 12% of General Revenue. In 2010, this dropped to 8.9%. In 2016, Corporate taxes accounted for 13.5% of General Revenue (total Revenue less Social Security and Medicare Payroll taxes as these should be Off Budget items). Now we hear that corporate taxes should be reduced further to a top rate of 15% from the now top rate of 35%. In the past few years we have learned that there are many corporations that pay no Federal Income taxes; this is unconscionable. Clearly, Corporations don't need more tax breaks. I recommend that corporations (and the wealthy) pay their fair share of General Revenue with the top rate of 35%. I have given examples on how this should be achieved. The tax otherwise paid by individuals would be converted to consumer spending. Since higher consumer spending would contribute to improving the economy, this idea deserves consideration. Corporations would benefit as this would increase their sales and profits resulting from the increase in demand for their products and services.

In the article, Fixing the Executive Branch, I recommended electing three Executive Administrators to manage many of the Departments and Agencies funded by Congress and managed by the Executive Branch. The objective was to obtain the required service at reasonable cost. This would also simplify the transition to a new Cabinet after a Presidential Election. Throughout my articles, I have made recommendations to reduce the cost of our Federal government while improving its effectiveness. The objective was to free up dollars to fund needed Federal program improvements.

America is the world's largest economy and the world's largest market. Everyone, individuals and corporations, want to participate in our economy and market. That is why we can charge a high tax rate. Any corporation wants to sell its products and services in the U.S. because the revenue and profit in the U.S. compared to other countries is so great.

Country	Revenue	Profit	Tax	After-Tax Profit
U.S.	$200m	$20m	35%	$13m
Other	$10m	$1m	10%	$0.9m

Clearly, the $13m After-Tax Profit (6.5%) is enough on $200m Revenue.

Note that the idea to reduce the maximum tax bracket to 15% instead of 35% only makes sense to provide greedy corporations and wealthy individuals with greater wealth.

The last years have shown that trickle-down economics (reducing income tax of individuals and corporations) doesn't work because corporations spend the extra income on executive bonuses, or buying back stock, and wealthy individuals spend the extra income on extravagant lifestyles.

The other aspect of taxes is that our government must spend approximately $1 trillion (without Social Security and Medicare) annually to operate our current government. Even with this large revenue, the country has large deficits every year, year after year, without our Congress taking corrective action. That is why we have such a large Federal Debt that is rising every year.

We don't want to waste taxes, instead we want to use taxes effectively. If we want a first-class government, we have to pay a first-class cost. This is particularly true for the Defense Department and Homeland Security.

When I mention Federal programs needing improvements, I am referring to programs such as our Federal Transportation System, our national Federal Highway System, our Defense Department, our Homeland Security System, etc.

Americans should be wary of politicians that pass spending bills or that pass income tax reduction laws that cause trillion-dollar deficits because the realistic anticipated revenue income is not sufficient to pay for these actions.

In the article, Fixing Federal Deficits and Federal Debt, I recommend a way to delete Deficits and at the same time reduce our large Federal Debt.

Below is a summary of the recommendations made to bring in needed revenue and reduce the Federal Debt and a summary of were the needed revenue is to be spent. Note that the summaries include a surplus of revenue of $100 billion. These are on an annual basis for the first year and for succeeding years.

Added revenue and reduction of Federal Debt

- Medicare Savings $238 billion

- R&D Tax Credit Repeal   150

- Capital Equipment Tax Credit Repeal   100

- Hedge Funds and Wall Street Fair Tax   112

- Estate Tax Reform   101.2

- Healthcare Savings   615.3

- Federal Debt Reduction   263

Total $1,579.5 billion

Below is where the needed revenue is spent

- Tuition-Free College $ 1.2 billion

- Deficit Reduction   600.0

- Debt Reduction   263.0

- Infrastructure Spending*   615.3

- Surplus**   100.0

Total $1,579.5 billion

*Six million jobs the first year and for years into the future.

** This surplus can be used to fund needed programs as outlined above.

I trust readers will evaluate that the recommendations are easy and fair and that they are possible and needed.

The $100 billion surplus above does not include all of the corrections required to have corporations and the wealthy pay their fair share of Federal income taxes. When all the corrections agreed to are made, the surplus will be greater than the $100 billion noted above. This will not only allow funding of needed programs, but could allow for a much needed tax reduction for Main Street.

I have often wondered whether the epitome (ideal example) of a successful capitalistic economy is one wherein corporations and wealthy individuals are the only ones that pay federal income taxes at a maximum rate of 35%. While this would mean they would keep a whopping 65% of their huge profits and large incomes, it would boost the economy by one trillion dollars of additional consumer spending thus further rewarding the corporations and the wealthy individuals. This is the opposite of the failed trickledown economics as it is based on proven consumer spending economic theory and is a win-win for all (the wealthy, the middle class and the poor). This would solve the unconscionable situation of the CEO's secretary paying more federal income taxes then her boss. Clearly, it is not a good idea to reduce the federal income taxes paid by the corporations and the wealthy, especially when we have large deficits and a large Federal debt.

In the article Fixing Federal Deficits and the Federal Debt, I reported on the legislation of 2010 regarding the extension of the Bush Tax Cut. Congress passed legislation providing tax cuts to corporations and the wealthy of one trillion dollars that year and for succeeding years. This resulted in the large increase in the Federal debt we see today, six years in the making. This trickle-down economy idea did not achieve jobs nor an improved economy. Now in 2017, Congress proposes a tax cut for corporations and the wealthy that will see the Federal Debt rise and that will not achieve jobs nor an improved economy. Make no bones about it, America should have a high tax rate for corporations that still leaves them with 65% of their profits because America has the best market in the world for corporations to be highly profitable. America does not need a low tax rate for foreign corporations to induce them to participate in our market or our economy.

12.SUBPRIME MORTGAGES

It is important that we understand subprime mortgages if we want to understand how Goldman Sachs and others caused a near depression (as we were told) caused by their selling flawed securities based on these subprime mortgages. You will be incensed as I was when I found out about these securities and the fact that they were allowed to be sold and no one responsible has gone to jail for this securities fraud. And don't believe the argument that laws are not in place to indict violators.

And don't believe the statement that subprime loans were a way to allow all Americans to reach the dream of home ownership. I am for this goal by making mortgages available with low down payments, but the ability to make monthly payments cannot be neglected in making loans. The truth of the matter is that subprime loans were driven by greed and irresponsibility on the part of the lenders and hurt Americans rather than helping them.

A 30-year fixed rate mortgage for a home purchase price of $365,000 would be $292,000 (with $73,000, 20%, down). At 5% interest, the monthly payment would be under $1,600. Let's compare this to a subprime loan.

	Down	Monthly	Balloon Payment	Total
Subprime	0	$2,500*	$30,000	$860,725*
30 Year	$73,000	$1,600	$0	$576,000

* Neglecting resets on the variable interest rate

Note that the subprime loan provided a 49% greater return than a typical 30-year fixed mortgage.

The subprime loans included both first and second mortgages each with interest rates several points above fixed 30-year mortgages and a balloon payment typically imposed on second mortgages. Note that where there is a foreclosure on the first mortgage, the second mortgage is typically worthless. This is one reason the securities based on subprime loans became such losers when foreclosures on subprime loans started (the first mortgage was first in line to be satisfied and typically the second mortgage was not in line to receive any reimbursement).

Note that after paying first and second loans for 30 years, a homeowner who has to pay a balloon payment of $30,000 to be able to own his home outright. I am sure that many homeowners were not made aware of this provision in their subprime mortgages. After paying principal and interest for 30 years, the homeowner could be foreclosed on if the $30,000 balloon payment was not paid in time after the end of the loan period.

I believe that Goldman Sachs and others knew that the subprime loans were doomed to fail. In fact, they got AIG to insure the securities so when they failed, they (Goldman Sachs) would be protected from loss (note that $60 billion of government aid provided to AIG went to Goldman Sachs to pay them for this insurance benefit). The securities rating agencies gave the securities a high rating and this aided Goldman Sachs to market them all over the world. From the above, the reader can understand how Goldman Sachs forecast high returns on the securities which made the securities attractive to investors (a $360,000 loan would return $860,725 in 30 years, a net gain of $500,724, 139%, almost two- and one-half times, over 30 years). As it turned out, the truth came out about the flawed securities and they became worth much less then investors had paid for them and in fact became unmarketable.

Note that our government failed the American people for letting all this happen and for not putting anyone in jail. In fact, our government gave money to these corporations who caused the problem in the first place (under the TARP Program). Don't believe that the government had no power to stop subprime mortgages or the issuance of the flawed securities and to put violators in prison. I am not talking about the cheaters who obtained false loans or the cheaters who inflated home prices, I am talking about the Goldman Sachs and others who sold flawed securities and the AIG's who issued flawed insurance that the government both bailed out. Instead of letting the violators suffer possible bankruptcy, the government let millions of Americans suffer foreclosures and let the economy fall into a recession. Also, Fannie Mae purchased these flawed mortgages and that put itself in a position that the government had to bail them out. If Fannie Mae had refused to buy these mortgages, the writers of these mortgages would have had less opportunity to pawn them off on others and that would have reduced this abusive practice.

The reader should realize that to keep funding available to the writers of these mortgages, that the providers of this funding had to have a way to sell them to create the availability of new funding for new mortgages. The providers of this funding also knew that these mortgages were flawed and that they could not hold on to them so they created the flawed securities backed by these risky subprime mortgages and sold these securities all over the world. As could have been predicted, foreclosures started and this house of cards fell down. This event dried up the funding availability of new funding causing the housing market to drop. This drop started foreclosures, increased unemployment and drove down the economy as the predicted credit crunch took effect. Once this cycle started, it affected a wider and wider circle of businesses, thus further increasing unemployment and driving down the economy. Unfortunately, our government failed the country and its people from the consequences. This could all have been prevented by the government promptly taking action as recommended to solve the foreclosure problem. Indeed, the government first recommended to buy these securities, but backed away from this plan. My opinion for this change is that the government would have had to cause institutions like Goldman Sachs to take the loss; the government takes the loss or a combination of the two.

If a buyer signed a subprime mortgage, we can assume that he/she accomplished some due diligence to check on house price comparables, various competitive mortgage offerings and his/her ability to make monthly payments. During the period of rising real estate prices, the homebuyer had reasonable expectations that he/she could refinance on favorable terms before the initial interest rate was reset.

However, the real estate bubble burst and home prices fell preventing the buyer from refinancing. The property was foreclosed when the interest rate reset and the buyer was unable to refinance or sell and could not afford the higher reset monthly payments.

Was the buyer at fault? No! He was aware of risk, but the unfortunate happened before his plan played out.

Was the mortgage company at fault? Yes! The mortgage company was not acting responsibly when it approved the loan without a down payment and not verifying that the buyer had the ability to pay. It was generally established that a buyer be given a mortgage that required the buyer to have the down payment and to have monthly expenses (including principal, interest, real estate taxes, Homeowner Association Fees and house insurance) not exceeding 34% of income.

Were the financial institutions (like Goldman Sachs) at fault? Yes! They sold the flawed securities based on the flawed subprime loans (a violation of the securities fraud law).

Was the government at fault? Yes! The government failed to protect its people against the unconscionable subprime mortgages, failed to protect investors from flawed securities and failed to prosecute violators. And instead of faulting violators, the government bailed them out and left Americans distressed with the drop in home prices, foreclosures, high unemployment, a recession and the unavailability of easy, low-cost responsible credit. The government's TARP, Stimulus Package and the Loan Modification programs have all been failures regarding helping Americans undergoing the distress. Yet corporations like Goldman Sachs were undeservingly saved.

Goldman Sachs and others are making high profits, paying high executive salaries and giving large bonuses. Clearly, the government did help them recover very fast, something not available to Americans in general.

Keep in mind that the problems with subprime loans hurt everyone since it curtailed the availability of funds for new mortgages and the drop in the housing market with the corresponding drop in home prices affected all Americans. Indeed, a credit crunch developed as the government warned us, but government efforts to stop the credit crunch has not been effective and the credit crunch persists to this day.

13. SOLVING THE FORECLOSURE PROBLEM

I recommend that mortgage companies allow lenders to stop paying the principal part of monthly payments for a year when homeowners get in a financial crisis while paying a fee of $500 to the loan company. The principal due and not paid would still be owed.

I also recommend that homeowners save a nest egg of a year's income to help them survive a financial crisis for a year. Homeowners should have a number of income avenues (part-time jobs for teenagers and spouse) and/or income from other sources as opposed to wages which may be lost.

The above recommendations should help to reduce foreclosures if the borrowers are able to survive the financial crisis.

I had suggested before the TARP Program was passed, that the government not buy the troubled securities but instead buy the underlying subprime mortgages (those that had not been previously foreclosed on). My recommendation to solve the foreclosure problem would work as follows.

The government would buy $1.1 trillion of subprime mortgages for $0.6 trillion. The $0.5 trillion difference is a loss (45%), but foreclosures would require higher losses to Goldman Sachs and others. This is probably equivalent to $1.3 trillion of securities because the financial institutions planned to make a profit on the securities (the $0.2 trillion, 11%, assumed here). However, I don't consider this $0.2 trillion a loss like the $0.5 trillion loss above but only the result of a failed (and flawed) business initiative that did not achieve the planned $0.2 trillion profit. Note that we are not asking the government to bail anyone out; we are asking financial institutions to take a loss. This loss is being extracted because these financial institutions did the wrong things by sponsoring subprime loans and then by selling flawed securities based on these subprime loans to unsuspecting investors. Readers need to realize that the drop in home prices have drastically reduced the value of subprime mortgages to the holders of these loans for the following reasons.

1.	The second mortgages associated with subprime mortgages are worthless because the home values do not cover the first mortgage as required for the second mortgage to have value. This supports the statement that sellers of these securities based on subprime mortgages committed fraud by misrepresenting their investment quality.

2.	The home values do not cover the first mortgage. You have been told repeatedly that many homeowners owe more on their mortgages than their home values.

3.	The widespread foreclosure problem in some areas has drastically reduced the value of foreclosed properties. Lenders will have significant losses associated with keeping foreclosed properties in saleable condition until they are auctioned off.

Essentially, subprime loans represent significant losses to the lenders. Therefore, lenders will need to seriously consider selling these loans to the government at a measured loss.

Unfortunately, the government is protecting the lenders by bailing them out and by allowing them to declare their losses over a long period of time. Further, the government is not helping homeowners who are the victims of these security frauds. My recommendations correct these injustices.

The financial institutions would have to take the deal offered or suffer the consequences. The institutions would be forced to take the loss immediately. This is in contrast to the government bailout which not only provided aid to help with immediate cash flow problems, but allowed these institutions to spread the loss into the future in order to protect their bottom line. Unfortunately, the government did not take this stand. Even if Goldman Sachs and others were forced into bankruptcy, there were others ready to step in and take their place in our financial markets.

When the assets of banks drop significantly due to the drop in values of mortgages held, the FDIC should consider taking over the banks for insolvency as is their responsibility to protect the depositors. This is done for small banks, but large banks are protected. The country has to quickly solve the foreclosure problem instead of letting it play out for years into the future without resolution.

The government would reduce each subprime mortgage by 40% (the drop in home prices) thus avoiding foreclosure and allowing the possibility of refinancing. The 40% reduction would leave the government with a profit of $60 billion. All of this could be done in a short time.

Total Subprime Mortgages	$1,100 billion
Purchase for	600
Reduced Mortgages	660
Profit	$60 billion

To obtain the 40% reduction, new mortgages would be restricted to traditional 30-year fixed rate loans for homeowner-occupied homes. There would be at least 10% equity. Therefore, the 40% reduction should be treated as a maximum to be lowered if necessary, to make things balance out.

Note that the government would be profiting from the refinanced mortgages resulting from the interest earned. At 4% interest on $660 billion of mortgages, the annual interest earned would be $26.4 billion the first year.

Over 10 million homeowners would be spared foreclosures, the mortgage business would bloom once again, the housing market will improve and Main Street would be in better financial shape. The objective is that jobs would be created, that the unemployment rate would come down and that credit availability would be restored leading to a healthier growing economy. Ten million foreclosures hurt everyone and must be prevented.

I would make this refinance available to small banks so that they could invest in good mortgages and make profits. I would hope that these small banks would sign up to helping themselves and their customers to have a secure future.

It is true that not all homeowners will be helped. However, these Americans should recognize that the $60 billion profit the government will make, the help in resolving the country's problem with subprime mortgages and the help to the economy will be worth it to all Americans.

While the country keeps suffering, Goldman Sachs and others continue to make high profits, pay high executive salaries, pay high bonuses and continue to be bad members of our society because they will not help with the credit crunch and the foreclosure problems which they created.

The government allowed Lehman Bros to go bankrupt, AIL bailed out with a $182 billion loan, CITI Group bailed out and seen Countrywide and Merrill Lynch purchased by Bank of America and Bears Stern and Washington Mutual purchased by J. P. Morgan Chase. Goldman Sachs and Morgan Stanley are still in business and striving. As of June, 2010, over 250 banks went under. Fannie Mae purchased subprime mortgages and got into a serious financial loss situation and has asked the government to bail them out. Everybody gets bailed out, except the homeowners.

One disgraceful part of the CITI Group bailout is that the government agreed to guarantee $306 billion of bad mortgage loans held by the CITI Group (the Treasury $5 billion, the FED $291 billion and the FDIC $10 billion). If you were the bank would you help a homeowner avoid foreclosure or would you let the government guarantee the bank from a loss? The distressed homeowner was not given relief.

Overall the government has committed $8.5 trillion to rescue Wall Street and the financial institutions, see below (as of November 2008):
$Trillions

	Total	Tapped
FED	5.6	2.1
FDIC	1.5	0.15
Treasury	1.1	0.6
FHA	0.3	0.3
Total	8.5	3.2

It is criminal to provide this level of aid to these organizations that caused the problems and to ask Americans to bear the pains and pay for the consequent Federal Debt and undergo the future shortfalls in the assets of the above agencies (FED, FDIC and FHA).

There have been suggestions about abolishing Fannie Mae and Freddie Mac. This is not a good idea because the country needs a source of cash to make mortgage loans and the government is the only one that can provide the large amount of cash required. The importance of this is that mortgages require that the money loaned be tied up in the loans and not available for other mortgages or other investments. For the private sector to prosper they need availability of cash. Mortgages don't provide this need. That is why we had the private sector package subprime mortgages into securities and sold them to get cash. The obvious answer is for Fannie Mae and Freddie Mac to continue. One advantage to Americans is that these agencies help make mortgages affordable. We cannot expect this from the private sector. Note that this is an example of the special interests increasing their efforts to obtain advantages for themselves thru heavily veiled recommendations that are offered as helpful to the people, but are only advantageous to themselves. All of this is due to their recent wins and the opportunity presented at this time with the campaign financing decision by the Supreme Court and the bitter battle between the two political parties to win and hold power. A reform is needed to require mortgage lenders to keep the mortgages they write and not pass them on to others. Banks have means to get cash from the Fed and this is a way for them to get cash to write additional mortgages. This would force lenders to operate with good practices or suffer the consequences. As an alternative, lenders could sell mortgages to Fannie Mae or Freddie Mac as has been the practice. But the mortgages would have to meet high standards. This would force lenders to follow high standards. Lenders would be prohibited from selling securities based on their mortgages. This is why it is necessary to continue with Fannie Mae and Freddie Mac. It is true that these agencies erred in buying flawed mortgages, but I doubt they did this knowingly. The lenders more likely lied about the quality of their loans. The government has been concerned about regulating financial institutions, but has not addressed the problem correctly. The government must advocate that financial institutions be responsible or suffer the consequences. No bail outs and no fraudulent securities based on bad collateral. Only good practices and high standards as recommended above. You can conclude that I am not for extensive regulation, only for strict accountability. This is why I have recommended the indictment of violators of security fraud. Since Fannie Mae and Freddie Mac hold nearly half of all mortgages (some $5-6 trillion), there is an opportunity for profits to be transferred to the government to help reduce the Federal Deficit and the Federal Debt. I realize that these agencies are not now profitable, but the opportunity exists for the future.

The special interests spin the information we are given and the media repeats this misleading information. We are told mortgage interest rates are at a low-time low. However, if you investigate, you will find that these rates include Points and are only available for loans below the conforming amount, available only to those with very low risk and carry very tight qualification conditions. The mortgage broker will switch you to a higher rate, because the advertised rate is only a teaser rate. This is hurting the solution to the foreclosure problem because refinancing is not available to those that still have some equity in their homes.

14. SOCIAL SECURITY AND MEDICARE

I present proof positive that Social Security and Medicare (Part A) can continue providing benefits through the year 2090 and beyond by simply capping the annual CPI increases to 2% as they effect benefits. The 2% is the goal set by the Federal Reserve for inflation. This statement is borne out by the Trustees own Low-Cost forecasts (with annual CPI increases set at 2%) so that this is the proof positive. (more on this later).

The reasons these programs are falsely forecasted to go into "insolvency" (the depletion of the surplus assets), is that the Trustees' forecasts are based on unrealistically high annual CPI increases of 2.7% (35% higher than the correct 2%) as they effect benefit increases and the Number of Beneficiaries in 2050 are based on unrealistically high forecasted Number of Beneficiaries of 97.3 million (30% higher than the correct 75 million) as they effect expenditures. The total incorrect effect of the two reasons is a false increase in total cost of 112% in 2050 ($5.3 trillion vs $2.5 trillion). These unrealistically high costs year after year in the future forecasts lead to false insolvencies. (more on this later).

The objective of this article is to gather public support to force the CBO to provide their own independent forecasts of the true financial future of these programs based on the simple solution presented. Because the people have lost their power of the vote and their power as consumers, recommendations are made to resolve these issues by the effective action of the people while not waiting solely for the CBO to act. Demonstrations don't work. Having accomplished this, it is hoped that the Justice Department will investigate for criminal charges against the Trustees for not acting to their required fiduciary duties and that the people will be able to silence the special interests that want to privatize these programs for their own profit motives. (more on this later).

There have been a large number of false statements sponsored by the special interests whose objective is to privatize these programs.

Let us discuss the false statements. The page numbers relate to the 2014 Reports for the year 2013.

The Reports are signed by the Secretary of the Treasury who is the Managing Trustee of these programs. Note that none of the Trustees spoke out about the false statements and that the media, nor our elected officials, never interviewed the Secretary nor the Trustees. Clearly, it appears that the media and the government are surrogates of the special interests and their lobbyists.

1. The Trust Funds are not real. The law requires that surplus assets be invested in securities guaranteed as to principal and interest and this law is followed (page 30). In fact, the Reports show that the securities are redeemed (the money borrowed by the government is being paid back to pay benefits as the surplus is depleted) (page 210). IOU's are used as a book-keeping tool to transfer

credits that are required to be used to invest in securities. At the end of 2013, the Social Security Trust had $2.8 trillion of guaranteed surplus assets. During the last recession, these programs did not lose a cent of principal nor interest, while private plans, like 401(k) plans, lost significant value.

2. Young Americans should not count on receiving benefits. The Reports show that income will always allow benefits. However, after the surplus is depleted, benefits will have to be reduced by approximately 25%. In 2050, maximum benefits are forecasted to be $49,529 in 2014 dollars (page 144). With a 25% reduction, the benefit will be $37,147. Note that these benefit numbers do not pass the test as being correct and therefore they should be verified by the CBO. Carrying out Note a, the correct Benefit would be $31,338 x 256.56 = $80,401 in 2014 dollars. Readers should understand that the pertinent benefit to review is the benefit in CPI-indexed 2014 dollars as this is the actual benefit payment forecasted taking into account that inflation will reduce the value of the dollar. The Report fails to list these figures. Note that benefits in the future are forecasted to be significantly higher than they are today.

3. The media irresponsibly repeated the special interest's false statement that the effect of the benefit reduction would be disastrous, stating that the average benefit in 2014 was $1,200 and that a 25% reduction would reduce this to $900. Since the reduction would not take effect until insolvency was reached in 2033, the facts are that a $4,493 maximum benefit in 2035 in 2014 dollars would be reduced to $3,370.

4. The program is a pay-as you-go program. With no savings, nor investments, this is a Ponzi scheme. This statement is false as clearly there are savings and investments. The $2.8 trillion of surplus assets at the end of 2013 (page 6) will allow paying scheduled benefits for over three years without collecting any income for that period of time (page 210). Therefore, it is not a pay-as you-go program and it is not a Ponzi scheme.

5. The government has to borrow money to pay benefits. The Treasury has chosen to pay benefits solely with the Payroll Taxes received, ignoring other sources of income. When Payroll Taxes are lower than benefits due, the Treasury redeems some of the surplus assets (securities) and the government is essentially borrowing money to accomplish these redemptions.

The benefits paid in 2013 were $812.3 billion. The Payroll Taxes received were $726.2 billion for a shortfall of $86.1 billion. The total income was $855.0 billion and the total expenditures were $822.9 for a surplus of $32.1 billion (page 6). Therefore, the statement that the program is spending more than it is taking in is false. The interest earned was $102.8 billion, which was $16.7 billion more than the shortfall. Therefore, if the Treasury paid the interest earned in cash it would not have to borrow to redeem securities to pay for the shortfall.

6. The programs are responsible for deficit spending. With no insolvencies, with no securities redemptions (without renewals) and with the elimination of all General Revenue funding, there will be no deficit spending. The solution presented avoids deficit spending of over $7 trillion in deficit (General Revenue) spending through 2033 with trillions more thereafter. This fact alone would call for the recommended solution. This issue of deficit spending has been misrepresented by the special interests who have stated that entitlement programs are responsible for huge deficit spending and that there exists a huge unfunded liability. Since securities don't need to be redeemed (without renewals) there is no unfunded liability to be concerned about because the money is owned, but does not require payment. In fact, the unfunded liability of the $18 trillion Federal Debt is of greater concern because China can redeem its securities and not renew them. The truth is that the programs can be made self-supporting, without any General Revenue deficit funding or unfunded liability, therefore there are no financial issues involving the continuation of these programs.

Turning to the Medicare 2014 Trustees Report, page 11, in billions, for the year 2013

Part	A	B/C	D	Total
Total Income				$575.8
Payroll Taxes	220.8	-	-	220.8
Interest	9.3	2.4	-	11.7
General Revenue	0.9	185.8	51.0	237.7
Premiums	3.4	63.1	9.9	76.4
Other	16.7	3.7	8.8	29.2
Total	251.1	255.0	69.7	575.8
Total Expenditures				582.9

Benefits

Hospital	136.8	41.8	-	178.6
Skill. Nurs. Facil.	28.4	-	-	28.4
Hom. Healt. Care	6.8	11.5	-	18.4
Physician	-	68.6	-	68.6
Part C	73.2	72.7	-	145.9
Prescription Drugs	-	-	69.3	69.3
Other	21.0	52.5	0.4	73.9
Total	266.2	247.1	69.7	582.9

For the year 2013, if the private plans of Parts C and D subsidized by the government were cancelled as will be recommended, the Part A results would end up with a surplus of $58.1 billion instead of a deficit of $15.1 billion. Part B/C would result with a surplus of $80.6 billion instead of a surplus of $7.9 billion, and the entire expenditure of Part D of $69.3 billion would be eliminated.

The average benefit per enrollee of $11,910 (page 11) would be reduced to $6,872.

7.   **The special interests have been stating that the high $11,910 average benefit per enrollee compared to the Payroll Taxes average collected per enrollee ($4,222, page 11) is the reason the program is in financial trouble. This statement is accurate, but misleading, because it doesn't acknowledge the total income and it classifies subsidies to private insurance companies as benefits. In fact, with the recommendations made, there is a huge surplus and the program has more income than it is paying out (see below).**

With changes recommended below, the average benefit per enrollee would be $6,872 vs the Payroll Tax (plus the total revenue) per enrollee of $8,166. This does not include the savings provided by the private pharmaceutical companies from the government-run prescription drug coverage program. Note the large surplus, $1,294 per enrollee, 19%, for 2013.

8.   For Medicare (Part A), the Low-Cost forecasts show large surpluses for every year after 2015 to the year 2090 and beyond. (page 65).

9.   Medicare Part B can be self-supporting by eliminating Parts C and D, adding a government negotiated prescription drug coverage program and collecting a small premium for the now free Part A which will be credited to the Part B.

From page 11

Income from General Revenue	$237.7 billion
Part C expenditures	145.9 (Private plans subsidized by the government)
Part D expenditures	69.3 (Private plans subsidized by the government)
Total Parts C and D	$215.2 billion (Versus $220.8 billion collected in Payroll Taxes

Total to eliminate General Revenue funding after elimination of Parts C and D: $22.5 billion

New Income

Part A Premiums Credited to Part B	$41 billion
Prescription Drug Coverage Premiums	36
Savings in Part B Premiums for Part C Overcharges	12
Subtotal	$89 billion

This yields a $66.5 billion surplus for Part B, while eliminating all General Revenue funding.

10.   The total surplus from Paragraphs 4, 6 and 8 would be $59.2 billion, 16.6%. Income would be $415.1 billion and Expenditures would be 355.9 billion. Note what a money-making program this would be.

The government negotiated prescription drug program has no deductible, no donut hole, no cap, no tiers and provides low cost drug prices. The monthly premiums will be less than $70 per month.

The elimination of Part C will end an ill-conceived program that is subsidized by the government and which adds significantly to deficit spending. Unlike private Supplemental plans, Part C places the insurance companies between the health providers and the patients and limits providers to those in the Networks. Medicare deficit General Revenue spending for Parts A, B, C and D is $237.7 billion versus the Payroll Tax and Premium income of $297.2 billion. This is why Medicare must be restructured so that it is self-supporting without any deficit spending and without any unfunded liability going forward. And that is precisely what the recommendations accomplish.

Medicare Part C (Advantage) is clearly an approach to kill Medicare and support the privatization of standard Medicare. Rather than provide needed extra benefits under standard Medicare, Part C gave the private insurers a way to compete with standard Medicare.

- Beneficiaries must give up their rights to standard Medicare and turn over the rights to private insurers to submit claims to standard Medicare, set up Network providers, collect government subsidies and submit Medicare claims that are 14% higher than standard Medicare.

- Private insurers were allowed to charge premiums (in addition to Part B premiums for standard Medicare paid by the beneficiaries), charge different deductibles and co-pays compared to standard Medicare with a loss of revenue to standard Medicare.

- Beneficiaries were forced to accept long waits for appointments, receive less quality medical care and have the insurer come between the provider and the patient.

- The government allowed private insurers to misrepresent Part C as a better choice within Medicare, provide additional coverage for dental, vision, hearing and gym membership (I would have preferred this additional coverage be added to standard Medicare and my recommendation allows for this added cost to standard Medicare).

11.   Premiums will go from $450 per month (Part B $100, Supplemental $260, Part D $90) to $250 (Part B $100, Part A $80, Part D $70) for a saving of $200 per month ($2,400 per year in savings).

Supplemental private policies are not a good choice because the annual cost of premiums ($3120) is far more than the average person can avoid for the costs not covered by Medicare ($1,499 Deductibles for Parts A and B, and twelve visits to doctors ($35 x 12=$420), for a total of $1,919).

12.   **It is recommended that the large surpluses be used to roll back the Normal Retirement Age, to roll back the Wage Cap subject to the Payroll Tax and that the Death Benefit be increased to pay for a decent burial for all Americans. To avoid financial problems for those Beneficiaries that incur large medical expenses, Catastrophic Coverage should be added. There should be little need for Medicare Supplemental Insurance thus reducing overall costs to Beneficiaries for these programs. Beneficiaries will also be saving on Premiums for Parts C and D. There will be savings due to the government negotiating prescription drugs prices. Note how a good program can be made much better by the simple recommendations presented.**

13.   The Trustees redeemed $270.45 billion of securities in 2013. (pages 155-156). Remember that only $86.1 billion of redemptions were required to cover the shortfall (see item 4 above). Of the total $270.45 billion redeemed, only $190.1 billion were redeemed of securities maturing in 2013. The balance redeemed ($80.35 billion) were redeemed of securities maturing in 2014 and thereafter. Therefore, there was a loss of interest. Since some of these securities redeemed before maturing had a higher interest than the renewals, again there was a loss of additional interest. **Americans should demand IOU's for this lost interest going back to 2008.**

14.   The special interests have been suggesting solutions that are not acceptable (e. g., increasing the Payroll Tax, raising the Normal Retirement Age, eliminating the cap on wages subject to the Payroll Tax, having the wealthy pay a higher Payroll Tax, imposing a means test to receive benefits, etc.). Their objective is to have Americans reject these distasteful solutions and settle for privatizing the programs. Medicare Part B premiums in 2016 will go up from $104.90 (in 2015) up to $389.80 for beneficiaries earning more than $428,000 (joint flier income) or more than $214,000 (single flier income). Medical expenses are not a function of income, therefore premiums for Part B medical benefits should not be a function of income. Note that this is a serious injustice.

15. Social Security is paid for by employers and employees, not by the government, as a Payroll Tax, paid with after tax dollars. This is very much like 401(k) plans, but these 401(k) contributions are not a Payroll Tax. Social Security is a pooled program where scheduled benefits not paid due to early death can be used to pay benefits for those that living longer. 401(k) plans are individual plans that pay only a cash balance while Social Security is a pooled plan that pays lifetime benefits. Social Security did not lose a cent of principal nor interest during the last recession, while most 401(k) plans took a significant loss. Social Security savings and investments are guaranteed as to principal and interest, while 401(k) programs carry no guarantees. Social Security administrative costs are very low while most 401(k) plans have high costs and fees and, due to the present economy, provide very small returns on principal invested.

I hope that readers will be incensed as I was when I researched the false statements being issued time and again without the media fact- checking, and, instead, the media repeating the statements as true. If you were a Trustee, would you not react to these lies? If you were an elected official would you not look into these allegations to verify that they were true? After all, the cost of Social Security in 2030 (when the last of the Baby Boomers have all retired, and some of the first to retire in 2012 start to pass), is forecasted as $2.2 trillion (page 214). This should be a peak in costs. The forecast for the cost in 2050 (when the last Baby Boomers have all passed) is $5.3 trillion in 2014 dollars (page 214). Why aren't these costs decreasing as the number of Baby Boomer Beneficiaries are being reduced after 2030? Why do costs increase to $12.8 trillion in 2070 (a 143% increase from 2050 to 2070) after the Baby Boomer era has passed and things should be returning to normal as the birthrate did after the Baby Boomer era? Clearly, it doesn't take a Rocket Scientist to smell that something is wrong. For the Low-Cost forecast the cost is $7.4 trillion in 2070 (not $12.8 trillion, a 76% increase). **The special interests stated that it was the increase in lifetime expectancy, which can be accepted as a real trend, but it is not the true cause. I could not believe that the Trustees published false forecasts. Violations of fiduciary responsibilities are criminal acts. I take this as criminal acts. I have taken the time to discuss these false forecasts so that the readers will know the truth.**

As the above research shows, the American people are not being given the truth, even though the truth is clear. Also, the American people are led to believe what they repeatedly are told to believe. These astounding statements point to flaws in our society resulting from actions by the special interests, their lobbyists and their surrogates (the media and our government).

I recommend national debates by college debating societies and writing of required laws and Constitutional Amendments by the law schools.

The Federal Reserve has stated that its primary objective is to keep inflation to 2%, or less, and to prevent long periods of high inflation that could damage the economy.

Yet the Trustees assume an unrealistic high annual increase of 2.7% for a very long period lasting 66 consecutive years, and compounded (pages 94-95). This results in the maximum benefit to reach $80,401 billion in 2050 in 2014 dollars and resulting in the value of a 2014 dollar to drop to 39 cents in 2050 (pages 144, 208). Clearly, this is what the FED wants to prevent. Clearly this is not a valid forecast. Therefore, the insolvency date forecasted is false. Note Item 2 above for a comment on the correctness of the benefit quoted here.

The Census Bureau forecasts the number of residents age 65 and above to be 88.5 million in 2050. Since the Normal Retirement Age will be 67 in 2022 and thereafter, and since all residents do not qualify for Social Security, the correct Number of Beneficiaries in 2050 is 75 million. Yet the Trustees forecast 97.3 million (page 57).

The Trustees Low-Cost forecasts are based on annual CPI increases of 2% and never reach insolvency through the year 2090 and beyond (page 210). This is based on a still too high 91 million Number of Beneficiaries in 2050. (page 58).

The Surplus assets for the Low-Cost forecast reaches $6.4 trillion in 2090 (page 210). With this large increase in surplus assets, the program could pay higher benefits than effected by the annual 2% cap on annual CPI increases as approved by Congress. Note what a successful program could result from the simple fix recommended. The maximum benefit in 2050 is $62,980 in 2014 dollars (pages 144, 209) with no reduction necessary to balance the budget. Note how the benefit of $62,980 compares to the Trustees forecast in 2014 dollars with the reduction ($60,301). The $60,301 is the $80,401 reduced by 25%. Note that the Low-Cost tabulation is mislabeled as the High-Cost tabulation on page 209. I am sure Americans will be relieved to find out that their maximum benefit in 2050 can be $62,980 in 2014 dollars. This is without Congress allowing a higher benefit because of the high surplus. See Item 2 above for a comment on the correctness of the benefits quoted here.

Below is a summary of the data in the 2014 Report (in 2014 dollars):

		Forecast (2.7% CPI)		Low-Cost Forecast (2% CPI)	
	2014	2050	Increase	2050	Increase
Cost	$0.86 trillion	$5.3 trillion	516%	$2.5 trillion	191%
Number of Beneficiaries	58.9 million	97.3 million *	65%	91 million *	54%
Max. Benefit Payment	$31,338	$80,401	157%	$62,980	101%

* The correct number is 75 million.

I have argued that the Forecast is false because of the high forecasted annual CPI increases and the high Number of Beneficiaries.

The 2050 costs ($5.3 trillion vs $2.5 trillion) validate the 112% increase in costs in 2050 between the Forecast and the Low-Cost Forecast stated in the second paragraph of this article.

Forecast stated in the second paragraph of this article.

Note that the unrealistic, high benefits forecasted confirms that the forecasts are not correct.

Be forewarned that the window to fix the problems is closing. In 2022, when Medicare starts to become insolvent and when the government is forecasted to start large deficit spending to redeem the large total surplus assets of $ 2.3 billion (page 210) thru 2033 (an average of $192 billion a year over 12 years, not including interest), there will be pressure to kill the programs. I can forecast that our media will tell the American people that this event was forecasted and that they should not be surprised as they were forewarned.

Because the programs will be self-supporting without any General Revenue funding and must meet balanced budgets, these programs should be moved to Federally-Chartered Corporations with Trustees from past Presidents who will select Executive Directors to run these programs. Clearly, the programs need better management. Depending on the success of better management, perhaps premiums can be reduced, providers can receive adequate payments for services and/or the Payroll Tax can be reduced (e.g., note that with the $66.5 billion surplus for Medicare shown above, the $41 billion of premiums for Part A could be eliminated).

I recommend Americans take action to save these programs. Americans need to follow the Iron Rule: Do onto others (the special interests) who have lied to take away Americans' retirement security with action on the peoples' individual right of choice to boycott, recognizing that individual action will be ineffective unless most Americans also feel hurt enough to also boycott. Boycotting is an easy way to bring required action and it will be effective as it is meant to provide financial stress in order that the special interests will correct their shameful actions against the people. If you hurt me by lying, prepare to be hurt by the truth and with boycotts to hopefully have you correct your actions. You disregard my welfare and I will have no forgiveness for you. Demonstrations don't work!

Please recognize the unbelievable, expansive, shameful, false and successful campaign waged by the strong special interests that must be defeated and commit yourself to accomplish the easy boycotts recommended to claim retirement security of all Americans. Unfortunately, organizations such as AARP and The Committee to Preserve Social Security and Medicare have failed to serve the American people.

Boycott the CBS Evening News (as a message to all media to provide the truth).

Boycott the retail products of the Koch brothers (Sparkle, Brawny, Vanity Fair, Angel Soft, Quilted Northern, Dixie, Marathon) as a message to all those that have sponsored the lies.

Boycott the services and products of GE and to others of the more than a dozen companies that have failed to pay Federal income taxes.

Boycott the services and products of Honeywell. Their CEO has led the Band of Sixty CEOs to campaign against entitlement programs. Yet it has been reported that his pension will be more than $50,000 per month. Let this be a message to all of Corporate America who want to eliminate these programs as an

objective to reduce deficit spending at the expense of eliminating the retirement security of all Americans and while not advocating for other better alternatives to reduce deficit spending.

The Chinese government requires American companies operating factories in China and employing Chinese workers to contribute to workers' pensions, medical care and housing. The housing benefit is meant to avoid the homelessness problem that is plaguing America. Yet there were special interests that recommended that American workers employed by American Auto Makers with factories in the U.S. to accept the lower wages and benefits of American workers employed by foreign counties operating auto factories in the U.S. Yes, there are those that are out to destroy the middle class in America and they must not be allowed to dominate.

Americans need to recognize that the special interests have already won as they have successfully achieved a widespread uncontested belief that the programs need to be privatized because they are financially unsound. All they have to do is persist until that 2022 date discussed above when the government will end the programs based on false data about the deficit spending and unfunded liability. This will validate the statements that the Trust Funds are not real and that younger Americans should not count on receiving benefits. My hope is that all Americans will take the actions recommended to prevent this and to restore retirement security to all Americans.

Don't allow Social Security to become a government Savings program benefiting financial institutions or allowing Medicare to become a government voucher program benefiting the insurance and pharmaceutical companies. Let's fight to keep these good programs and make them better with the recommendations presented.

Let us not lose sight that this can be the start of a new era wherein the people regain lost power and that that brings forth more of a government of the people, for the people and by the people. We can identify problems, propose good solutions and have these solutions instituted by using the powers of the people.

Hundreds of thousands of Americans united behind the boycotts is the only way that the 1% special interests, their lobbyists and their surrogates can be neutralized

15.TRADE

Americans are being misled about trade agreements.

Countries that pursue trade vigorously do so to create jobs and improve the economy in their country. And some countries are very aggressive in trade deals in order to get the best deal. They subsidize their products in order to export high quality products at very, very low prices to dominate world markets. They steal technology and require trade secrets from foreign companies that want to establish factories in their country and they impose tariffs to deter imports and thus protect their industries. This is not a complete list of factors that must be dealt with in establishing trade deals. It is why free trade has its problems because bad practices are difficult to control.

Americans need to understand that trade among countries can be good for both countries. An example is an agreement between the United States and Chile to trade in the flower business. Since the two countries have opposite growing seasons each country can benefit by sharing growing seasons. Of course, there are conditions that must be met involving all regulatory issues. The same can be said for trade involving fruits and vegetables. Note that American Importers, Wholesalers, Retailers and consumers all pay taxes on these imported goods. Also, note that each country improves its job category because a seasonal market is converted into an annual market.

Each country selects three importers and three exporters to handle the trading.

Note that the Trade Balance is a result of many agreed-to factors and there may need for one country to subside their industry while the other country charges a tariff on imports in order that consumer prices are fairly stable throughout the year and that profits remain fairly stable and reasonable throughout the year in both countries.

Each country must guarantee that the trade doesn't affect the viability of its own industry and the job situation associated with its own national industry. Therefore, countries must be allowed not to participate in free trade on free-trade that impacts the viability of its own industry and the job situation associated with its own national industry.

Americans need to address the issue of a company closing its plants in the United States and moving them and/or the company headquarters to other countries to lower labor costs and/or to avoid paying United States income taxes. This is not a trade issue. My solution is not tariffs, but prohibition of their products and services not be allowed to be sold in this country. If "Free Trade" doesn't allow this prohibition, then "Free Trade" is not fair. In some cases, tariffs are in order if negotiated. The key is a good deal, fairly negotiated between two parties.

Trade between countries need not be covered by trade agreements. The U.S. is one of the world's biggest producers of agricultural products and this results in opportunities for a large export business. On the other hand, The U.S. finds it necessary to restrict the import of foreign sugar in order to protect its own sugar industry.

Countries must be allowed to take steps not to be dependent of a foreign government for vital supplies, such as oil. On the other hand, it must be acknowledged that some foreign countries provide the only source of an item, such as Africa in Cocoa beans for Chocolate products.

I believe that the move of foreign automobile companies (Toyota, BMW, Honda, etc.) to build plants in the U.S. and hire American workers is a good idea. I would insist that these companies pay income taxes on the profits of these U.S.-based subsidiaries and that they reciprocate by allowing American automobile companies to build plants in their countries and/or allow American automobile companies to sell their products in their countries without tariffs.

The key is that the U.S. is the best market in the world and that all foreign companies want to address that market. Therefore, America has a strong position to negotiate from. However, countries need to avoid trade wars.

In summary, it is obvious that a broad Free-trade agreement between countries or among countries is not in anyone's best interest and that trade agreements must be accomplished on a specific item between a specific country in order that all the complex effects can be covered. Any trade agreement should be approved by Congress

16. Fixing the Immigration Crises

The immigration problem is very complex so that readers need to recognize that an easy solution is not evident. However, the problem needs to be solved and the inaction of our government is unconscionable.

The immigration crisis stems from the fact that many foreigners desire to enjoy the benefits of living in our country.

Americans need to decide who can get an opportunity to apply for residency and the process for approval or disapproval.

Americans need to eliminate illegal immigration and increase penalties therefor. It is not a solution to simply require detention and deportation.

Americans need to make it extremely difficult for illegals to live in our country without legal status. Therefore, it is unconscionable that we tolerate 11 million illegal immigrants to live in this country without concern. No wonder others try to join these 11 million.

Clearly, our broken government refuses to resolve these difficult issues. The strong force that has been guiding me has not provided much guidance to date. Perhaps, recommended solutions and laws will have to come from the America Corps and perhaps they will be able to use the recommended process to establish solutions and laws voted on by the state legislatures.

One issue that I recommend Americans consider is the plight of the eleven million illegals presently residing in our country.

It has been estimated that in 1990 there were 3.5 million illegal immigrants living in the US. In 2007, this peaked at 12.2 million then dropped to approximately 11 million and the 11 million has been stable for the last 11 years at 11 million ever since.

In 2014, 75% of illegals living in the US (8.25 million) had been living in this country for more than a decade, and only 5% came to this country over the previous 5 years.

This tells me that special interests (the powerful companies and the wealthy) want to do nothing about the illegals living in this country because they are able to hire these immigrants at low wages and thus fatten their own pocketbooks.

Over the years, I hired Hispanics as gardeners, handy people, house cleaners, etc.

I hired them through referrals and I never investigated whether or not they were illegals. Sometimes they were employees of legitament business I contracted with. I was never disappointed with the service I received.

Therefore, I recommend we address what should be done about these 11 million illegals. The country cannot advocate for the elimination of illegal immigration unless it eliminates the large number of illegal immigrants living in the country.

If the number of illegal immigrants has been stable at 11 million for 11 years, there is not a crisis of an invasion. If there have been no problems with these 11 million illegal immigrants for 11 years, there is not a security problem. However, again, the country cannot advocate for the elimination of illegal immigration unless it eliminates the large number of illegal immigrants living in the country.

I stress that the recommended solution is "fair" because the recommendations follow the rules and laws of the land. I also stress "fair" because a portion of the fault for the present situation rests with our government actions and lack of actions. The government allowed the number of immigrants to rise from 3.5 million to 11 million, and as we will point out, has violated their constitutional rights.

As always, I ask for national debates and national polling to arrive at what the people desire.

The story starts with the plight of many people outside of our borders that wanted a better life for themselves and their families and saw the opportunity to have a better life in our country. As it turned out, the U.S. did not take adequate steps to stop the large flow of immigrants illegally crossing our borders and settling in our country or overstaying their visas. This shortcoming by our government resulted in many foreigners taking the chance to enter the country illegally and face the punishment of deportation.

I don't need to relate the hardships and challenges the immigrants endured in crossing the border and living in their new country. Yet, they persisted because they believed in the promise for a better life for themselves and their families provided by America. The proof is that existence of tens of millions of illegal and undocumented immigrants in the country has not been a safety issue.

The undocumented immigrants were able to get jobs because business found that they could hire these immigrants for low wages and eliminate the need to pay the higher wages demanded by American workers. We all witnessed the lack of suitable clerks and services as layoffs of American workers occurred and as this change brought on the change in the ethnicity of employees in low-paying and low-status jobs that Americans would not take. Yet for the majority of immigrant workers, they appreciated the jobs and did not complain. In retrospect, the immigrant workers provided a needed service. While it became illegal to hire undocumented immigrants, the special interests were successful in retaining their workers and their low, stagnant wages by avoiding a solution to the Immigration crises.

The irony is that the Constitution guaranteed citizenship to all born in this country. Let me hasten to state that this guarantee should be redefined so that it is not taken advantage of. What the government should do is provide this guaranteed citizenship to those born in this country. This will drastically reduce the number of undocumented immigrants in the country. The rules of the Immigration Department are that parents of these children and the siblings of these children are given Permanent Residency (Green Cards), and having met strict requirements, again reducing the number of undocumented immigrants in the country. I don't know how to calculate the reduction in the number of undocumented immigrants living in this country by this action, but it could well be in the multiple millions.

I am very disappointed when I see on TV that a mother of children born in this country is being deported. Constitutional rights are being violated and the rules of the Immigration Department are being violated. And more to my disappointment, the Supreme Court doesn't protect the Constitutional rights.

When these children are of age, some twenty years or so after birth, the parents and siblings should be considered for, but not guaranteed, continued green cards if they meet strict requirements.

The government should provide, but not guarantee, Permanent Residency (Green Cards) to workers that have a long history of honorable work and meet strict requirements. This also will reduce the number of undocumented immigrants in the country. In fact, if only half of the 8.25 million having lived in the US for more than a decade in 2014 were granted green cards for honorable work history and having met other strict requirements, the reduction in undocumented immigrants would be 4.125 million.

The following are also required to fix the immigration crises:

- Secure the border (with manpower and technology, but without a wall over the entire border)

- Deport immigrants who have broken our laws

- Provide undocumented immigrants with standard ways to receive Green Cards and/or Citizenship (with compliance with the laws and procedures):

    The following also requires meeting other strict requirements.

    Thru honorable work history

    Thru job offers

    Through Investment

    Through job creation

    Armed Forces Member

    Spouse of a U.S. citizen

    Unmarried children under age 21 of a citizen

    Parents of a U.S. citizen

    Children born in this country

    Parents and siblings of children born in this country

The government should solicit volunteer citizens to provide aid to undocumented immigrants to apply for the above avenues to secure Citizenship and/or Green Cards.

I do not agree that young children brought into this country illegally by their caregivers should be given protection from deportation nor should their caregivers also receive protection. We must adhere to the law for past and future offences.

Illegal immigrants without documentation should be deported after the above proper remedies are complete.

Hopefully, the undocumented immigrants that cannot obtain Citizenship nor Permanent Resident status and find jobs will self-deport. The improving job availability in Mexico would make this prudent.

I fault the Supreme Court for not upholding the Constitutional rights of those born in this country and for the lack of proper action for their parents and siblings. I also fault our Congress and the Executive Branch for their bad actions and their lack of effective action.

Readers should reflect on historical precedents that residents of the territories involved with the Louisiana (including Oklahoma) Purchase, the Alaska Purchase and the territories involved with the Mexican-American wars were granted citizenship without any action on their part.

I have found immigrants living in this country very family oriented and of good character. I remember a Hispanic tow truck driver telling me that he had the best job in the world because he was constantly put in a position of helping people in desperate need for help and that he could provide that help. I have also found these immigrants appreciative of having jobs and with an attitude to do the best job possible for their employers to keep their jobs.

Americans should demand that a minimum wage law be passed, that an overtime law be passed and that employers who have hired undocumented workers be fined for breaking the law. I would suggest that Americans boycott Carl's Jr. And Hardee's fast food chains as a message to all employers that they cannot break the law on hiring undocumented immigrants and that they must treat their employees fairly.

The government should accomplish the following to deter the number of illegal, undocumented immigrants in the country.

Stress the importance of legal avenues to enter the country

Eliminate immigrants overstaying their visas

Educating Americans on not giving employment or other aid to illegal immigrants

Eliminating public or private aid to illegal immigrants

The above is to make it impossible for illegal, undocumented immigrants to survive in our country. The objective is to deter immigrants from entering the country illegally and to foster self-deportation.

The following make a solution difficult:

America is a destination coveted by many

Illegal immigration is difficult to eliminate entirely

Illegals must find it impossible to stay in this country

Legal immigration needs to be the acceptable path

The penalty for illegal immigration must be more than detention and deportation

Illegals should not be hired and tough penalties should be imposed

17. Providing Tuition-Free College Education

Our country has excellent colleges and universities (public and private). These institutions draw students from all over the world. However, there are three problems:

- The high cost

- The limited enrollment availability

- The student loan problem

A specific example is UCLA, the public university of the State of California in Los Angeles, that has the following shortcomings:

- It has limited enrollment capacity

- It typically rejects many deserving and qualified local and California-wide students while accepting many out-of-state and foreign students

- Its costs are high

- Many students have to resort to student loans

Clearly, UCLA is not even capable of accepting deserving and qualified students even when they are paying full tuition. Much less if tuition were free.

Clearly, there is no way UCLA can be made Tuition-Free and enroll and support   the large number of local and state-wide qualified students who would want to take advantage of the superior college education available from UCLA. The same can be said for other public and private colleges and universities.

I do not recommend that we destroy our current high-quality colleges and universities, public or private.

The politicians that promise Tuition-free college education (even though they limit this benefit to community colleges) are simply catering to the voters with a promise that they cannot deliver on. And this is discrimatory because it is limited to community colleges. However, as is discussed below, there is a solution that can provide tuition-free education without destroying our present superior educational system. In fact, as we will explain below the solution has the promise that it can improve our present educational system which is a must needed necessity. This approach is similar to that recommended for healthcare insurance that provides a solution without destroying our superior healthcare system. Let me restate here that our government has been supporting the Healthcare Insurance and Pharmaceutical companies by placing them between the patient and the doctor and providing lower quality healthcare through a network system that is high in demand, but low in availability and low in quality of healthcare and which is high cost and unaffordable without large government subsidies.

If we are to find a solution for tuition-free college, we must develop a strategy that will solve the shortcomings listed above for present public and private colleges and universities (the high cost, the limited enrollment and the student loan problem). At the same time, we need to provide for a top-quality education. If we achieve these goals, we will not only help succeed with a viable tuition-free college opportunity, but also incentivize present institutions to improve by solving their shortcomings.

Readers should recognize that there is a real problem to be solved. Tuition-Free college education is not possible and the high cost of college tuition and fees is too high, leaving a huge gap as who can attend college.

The principle that should guide us is that everyone should have the opportunity to attend college. With this principle in mind, we arrive at the fact that our young adults in the inner cities lack the opportunity to attend college or vocational training for many reasons which we will discuss and remedy.

The recommendation is to develop a separate venue as follows:

- Establish a tuition-free college in South Central Los Angeles, California (this can be emulated in other inner cities across the country)

- Use the available Sears buildings and grounds (hopefully this will be a donation for college-naming rights)

- Recruit the best administration and faculty and paying top salaries.

- Pay for the operating costs by Federal funding and private contributions.

- Students to be provided with backpacks, books, computers, etc. at no cost, hopefully these will come from donations.

- The operation to be a public institution of the City of South Central that is removed from today's bureaucracy.

- Enrollment granted to all students of South-Central meeting enrollment standards. Enrollees must reside in the City, have attended three years of City High Schools and graduated the current year or two years before current year.

- Institution providing both academic and vocational training.

- Institution to be tied-in with employers to promote graduates with the correct training and numbers of graduates to promote job availability after graduation.

- Students receiving these benefits have no obligation to pay back benefits

- No students who are not residents for the required period will be provided enrollment. The goal is to become the top college or university in the country and the world in terms of percent of freshmen graduating on schedule, percent of graduates getting job offers and average starting salary of job offers.

To achieve the above goal, the local schools need to be improved to provide a college prep curriculum. Students need to be helped to prepare for college and to select a major.

The remaining problem is funding. If the maximum number of students is 12,000, then the annual cost will probably be $60 million. This can be provided by adjustment of the Federal Estate Tax. The 2010 Compromise on the extension of the Bush Tax Cut reduced Estate Tax revenues by $88 billion annually. Because of this change, the Estate and Gift Tax revenue for 2011 was only $7 billion. The adjustment in the law could easily bring more than the required $1.2 billion annually (for 20 colleges) the first year and for years into the future. In 2016, the total General Revenue from Estate and Gift taxes was $21 billion, more than the $1.2 billion required by this recommendation (this without the change in the Estate tax). However, the wealthy has been receiving the $88 billion reduction, and more, annually since 2010, and the law should be changed so that the wealthy pay their fair share of Estate taxes. This added revenue is to pay for this program and for other programs that are needed by the country and its people. I estimate that there will be added surplus revenue of $100 billion to spend on programs critical to our future and the future of our country.

Note that other inner cities programs would only be approved after the initial site was proven to meet expectations.

Note that if Congress passes the initial funding of $60 million, there will be surplus funding the first year and for the subsequent three years for facility, operating costs and preparation improvements as follows:

Year	Enrollment	Operating Costs	Funding	Surplus
–	0	0	$60m	$60m
1st	3,000	$15m	$60m	$45m
2nd	6,000	$30m	$60m	$30m
3rd	9,000	$45m	$60m	$15m
4th	12,000	$60m	$60m	0

Note that facility improvement, enrollment and start of classes are all on a fast track. Classes start the second year.

I want readers to recognize that I recommend that the portion of the new Estate tax to be reserved for this Tuition-Free College Education Program (i.e. $1.2 billion annually, the first year and for years into the future). The funds should be placed in a Trust and invested as is the case for Social Security.

If the new Estate Tax would be changed to provide a $3 million Tax-Free amount and the balance subject to ordinary income taxes, a $100 million estate would yield $66.05 million after taxes and bring in more needed revenue to the government.

Keep in mind that the recommendation helps solve the following national problems:

- Tuition -Free College Education for the most needy

- Helps inner-city areas to prosper as property values will increase

- Helps close the income-equality gap

- Helps reduce poverty

- Helps reduce crime in the inner cities

- Helps fixing Federal deficits and the Federal debt by increasing revenue to pay for the program by reforming the Estate Tax law.

- Helps fixing the Economy and creating jobs

Perhaps the recommendation will have an effect on present colleges and universities to reduce their cost of education while providing a high-quality education.

There are a number of areas where revolutionary thinking and action are required. The objective has to recognized as one that graduates superior graduates at affordable cost and having job offers available.

Graduates need to be evaluated by employers as superior compared to other colleges and universities in selected fields. Rather than offering many types of degrees, the institution should concentrate on perhaps only Business and Education. These are the main driving forces in our society. Perhaps these degrees should be five or six years and include some work experience.

Another area is the enrollment process. Candidates should be prepared to enter college or vocational training. This places responsibility on local high schools.

Another area is the support process. Because the enrollees come from low-income areas, many students will require support in nutrition, grooming, attire, relationships, studying, financial aid, etc.

112